California in Color

Hans W. Hannau

California in Color

112 full-color photographs

Distributed by

DOUBLEDAY & COMPANY, INC.
GARDEN CITY, NEW YORK

Library of Congress catalogue card number 77-78667.
Printed in Austria.

INTRODUCTION

In California there is an assortment of celebrations with strong ethnic overtones that enchant the residents.

In San Francisco, the Chinese New Year is a gaudy pageant, celebrated in February with a giant paper-dragon parade and snapping firecrackers.

By summer, Solvang turns the Santa Ynez Valley community over to Danish Days, with heady offerings of folk music and dancing and boggling heapings of Danish food.

September in San Pedro sees the Fishermen's Fiesta, when the Portuguese and other fisherfolk decorate their diminutive boats and parade them offshore.

According to the season, near the Mexican Olvera Street in downtown Los Angeles, a priest conducts the traditional Blessing of the Animals.

Likewise, in December, at Padua Hills near Claremont, the Mexican Christmas festival Las Posadas is staged.

Each celebration is a visual experience, each has a particular significance, usually an expression of joy. Yet in each of these fêtes and festivals California itself is being saluted, for California is the state of mind that makes it all possible. The Chinese, the Danes, the Portuguese, the Mexicans, all are historically woven into the fabric of colorful California, and when these special groups stage their holidays all California watches and enjoys.

This fabric of California—call it a patchwork quilt—is made up of contrasts: green lawns by January, fields of holiday poinsettias, orange groves, tidal salt flats stalked by birds, shining desert pavement, ruddy redwood forests, white beach sand, white desert sand, color, color, contrast and color.

California is a visual experience, overwhelming at times, reassuring at others. It is sweep and bulk and expanse and distance, and more. It is sweet Sierra wind, and it is perfumed fog that marches inland at Marin and Monterey and San Simeon. It is a hot desert-born wind that scrubs out the seaward canyons and flattens billboards. It is miles of cotton, fat-bolled and prosperous; it is purple grapes hanging in bunches as long as a man's forearm; it is windrows of fresh-cut alfalfa and endless bright gardens of gardenias and camellias and azaleas.

People have come to California for more than a hundred years and will continue to come because of the serenity of the deserts, the peace of the beaches, the madness of the beaches, the remote grandeur of the mountains, the incredible freeways, the lonely paved byways that know only two cars in a given day.

Poor indeed is the man who comes to California seeking only the artificial, the glitter of Hollywood, the plywood charm of movie sets.

California's visual charms are without number: the natural wonders, the historical structures, the fields of harvest, the long sky.

No wonder the paths into California are clogged with a thousand new arrivals a day.

Easterners are charmed by California's smiling climate. No snow, no sleet, no iced winds. Smog—which also exists in other states—is annoying; but Oklahoma knows cyclones and North Dakota knows incredible chills.

The cities of California ask visitors to call again. The major cities have endless wonders: San Diego, San Francisco, Los Angeles.

But the little communities also beg you to tarry awhile. Visit San Juan Bautista, Sausalito, Columbia, Volcano, Alleghany, Carmel, Julian, Bridgeport, Markleeville, and reckon with their charms.

California knows all races and roots of races. The Spanish and the Mexicans and the Indians all enroll in the same school. The Gold Rush, the land booms, the lyric of California enticed argonauts from all over the world and they have found the land fair.

It is a land of reason and unreason, of the gaudy and the restrained, of many religions and of no religions, of bright colors and, above all, of contrast. California is tall enough or green enough or rhapsodic enough to charm the senses of most who call.

California offers a vast variety of scenery. The chief geographical divisions in the north are, from west to east, the coastal lowlands, the Coast Range, the Central Valley, and the tall Sierra Nevada that forms the eastern mountain rampart of the state.

In the south, from west to east, one finds the coastal plain of the Los Angeles Basin, the numerous walls of the Coast Range, the Valley of Southern California, the transverse network of the San Gabriels, the San Bernardinos and other mountain ranges, and finally the arid regions of the Mojave and Colorado Deserts in the southeastern hinterland.

The California shore extends for almost a thousand miles, from the Oregon border to the Mexican frontier, flanked by the coastal mountain range, which runs parallel to the shore. The region from Oregon to San Francisco is a thinly populated area covered with woods or exposed grazing lands. The dramatic redwood forests, many of whose trees were centuries old when Christ was born, stand from the sea edge to a few miles inland. Towns and villages are few, and the traveler can ride miles without seeing a sign of human habitation. It is only when one approaches Marin County that one encounters the first major populated area in California. South of San Francisco are the attractive seaside cities of Santa Cruz, Monterey, and Carmel, with its art colony. Below Carmel is the rugged beauty of the Big Sur country, where the highway clings to cliffs, often shrouded in fog. The main north-south highway, however, runs inland beyond the coastal mountains.

From the moment the traveler reaches the charming and wealthy city of Santa Barbara, the Pacific shoreline becomes more thickly populated. A series of built-up areas continues all the way down to the Mexican border city of Tijuana, 225 miles to the south.

Here are the well-known cities of Ventura, Oxnard, Santa Monica, Los Angeles, Long Beach, Laguna Beach, Oceanside, La Jolla, and San Diego. Here, too, is a concentration of California's beaches, boating areas, fishing facilities, trailer parks and, in places, oil wells.

Inland from the coast, northern California is a country of great primitive forests and beautiful mountains. There are no large cities in the area. The region is noted for its hunting and fishing, its lumber camps and mills.

6

The food basket of California lies in the state's adjoining inland valleys, which stretch a distance of 425 miles. These are the Sacramento Valley and the San Joaquin Valley, enclosed by the Coast Range on the west and the Sierra Nevada on the east. The latter range separates this lush agricultural Central Valley from the upper Mojave Desert. The valleys offer miles of flat, fertile, and flourishing fields of agricultural products, sufficient to fill all the tables of the country.

The capital of California, Sacramento, is situated in the northern part of the Central Valley. Fresno stands midway in the valley. At the southern end is the fast-growing city of Bakersfield. Oil wells and cotton fields nearby contribute to Bakersfield's prosperity. South of Bakersfield are the Tehachapi Mountains.

HISTORY

When the first white men arrived in California in the sixteenth century, they found friendly people singing and dancing. The native population of the Pacific coast had lived along the shores and in the valleys for at least three thousand years, in isolated villages and largely without tribal ties. From the beginning of man's time, it would seem, Californians were of widely diverse origins. The California Indians spoke more than a hundred dialects of twenty-one distinctly different languages.

Their houses were often round huts covered with bark, thatch, or poles. Kitchen middens of shell, ash, and earth piled up over centuries testify to a very simple culture and a sea-food diet along the coast. The Indians ate birds, small game, and insects. In most parts of the state, acorns were a staple food. Acorn meal was made by drying and grinding the acorns and leaching out the tannic acid with many soakings in water. It was baked in cakes or eaten as a mush. In the southwest the Indians ate mesquite beans, and on the mountain slopes they gathered piñon nuts. Along the Colorado River they raised plants for food. They wove baskets, chipped arrowheads, and fashioned pestles, mortars, and beads from stone. They made whistles and flutes from bone. They were waterborne on rafts and in plank canoes.

The man who named California never saw it. He was Hernando Cortes. In 1535 he landed on a rugged peninsula which he thought was an island, in what is now Mexico. The Spanish conquistador was familiar with a popular Spanish romance of 1510, "The Exploits of Esplandin," which makes mention of a fictional California as "an island rich in gold," very near the Terrestrial Paradise. Hence Cortes named that Pacific shore California. Cortes's California is now Baja California.

In 1542, a new Spanish viceroy sent Juan Rodriguez Cabrillo, a Portuguese navigator, on an expedition to examine the western side of California as far northward as possible. He was the first white man to land on the soil of what is now the State of California when he entered a very good closed port, the bay of San Diego. Northward from there his ships passed the Golden Gate without seeing it. On San Miguel Island, Cabrillo supposedly died and was buried.

Not until Francis Drake rounded Cape Horn in his 100-ton schooner, the *Golden Hind,* did Spain show any more interest in California. Drake careened his ship north of San Francisco in 1579. He reported that the Indians asked him to become their king. He named the region New Albion and claimed it for England.

Spain was stimulated thereby to make more thorough explorations of the coast. Sebastián Vizcaíno in 1602 named the first harbor he reached San Diego and also christened other landfalls—Santa Barbara, Santa Catalina, Point Conception, the Carmel River, Point Reyes, and Monterey Bay. Settlers, soldiers, and Jesuits were placed along the eastern coast of the Gulf of California in 1683 in an effort to stimulate the pearlfishing industry.

In the midseventeenth century, another foreign power suddenly began to take more than a passing interest in California—Czarist Russia. Russian fur traders and explorers had traveled all the way down the coast from Alaska to the Farallon Islands off San Francisco. When the Spanish government got wind of the Russian Czarina's intention to settle California, it wasted no time in dusting off the old projects for colonizing the area.

Twin expeditions were arranged. These were to be dispatched from Lower California (Baja California) to secure the country and to convert the Indians. One group was to proceed by sea and the other by land. The plans were drawn up by the King of Spain's personal agent in New Spain, Inspector-General José de Galvez. Don Gaspar de Portolá was placed in charge of the expeditions. Under him, in charge of the missionaries, was Father Junípero Serra.

The sea party suffered incredible hardships en route to San Diego. Of the three ships that sailed for Upper California (Alta California), one was lost, and a large part of the crews of the other two died of scurvy. The overland contingent did not fare so badly.

On July 16, 1769, Father Serra was able triumphantly to raise the cross on the site of the first mission in California. This was called the Mission San Diego de Alcalá.

Two days before the mission at San Diego was dedicated, Portolá set out by land to occupy the port of Monterey, the basic purpose for which his expedition had been commissioned. Thus, he was the first white man to outline part of the route of El Camino Real—the Royal Way—between San Diego and Monterey. It was on this historic route that Father Serra would start the construction of his famous and romantic chain of missions which were to be the first outposts of civilization in California.

THE MISSIONARIES

To understand the importance of the missions in the history of colonial California, it is necessary to know something of the indomitable spirit of the missionaries who helped to found them. Among this heroic, dedicated, and passionately religious group of Franciscans two personalities emerge—Father Junípero Serra and Father Fermín Lasuén.

Serra was the first Father-President of the California missions. He is considered the establisher of Christianity and founder of civilization in California. A native of Mallorca (born 1713), he joined the Franciscans at the age of seventeen. His apostolic career began in 1749, when he set sail for America. He was never again to see his native land. For almost twenty years he labored in Mexico, mostly in the Sierra Gorda regions, before undertaking the establishment of the missions of Alta California and the evangelization of the area. Father Serra rode 750 miles on muleback up the peninsula of Baja California and into San Diego despite a badly infected leg. After he had established the mission at San Diego, he went on to found eight more: San Carlos (1770), San Antonio (1771), San Gabriel (1771), San Luis Obispo (1772), San Francisco (1776), San Juan Capistrano (1776), Santa Clara (1777), and San Buenaventura (1782). He made his headquarters at his beloved mission San Carlos, at Carmel, where he died in 1784. His remains are still there.

Father Serra was the incarnation of the virtues of the Franciscan order. Lean, ascetic, devoted to duty, and possessing immense physical courage, he was a priestly missionary of some administrative ability. At the same time, he was humble and self-sacrificing and represented the very antithesis of the cupidity, arrogance, and lust for material wealth that characterized many of the secular settlers. He is, in fact, commemorated by statue and tablet in more than two hundred places in the United States, Mexico, and Spain. The church is at present discussing the possibility of declaring his sainthood.

When Father Serra died, the building of the mission chain passed on to his successor, Father Fermín Lasuén, who carried forward Father Serra's dream with great skill and energy. Before he died, Father Lasuén had added nine more missions to the chain. He was a man of enormous executive and administrative talent. Indeed, the operation of eighteen missions called for extraordinary efforts on his part. Many authorities claim that Lasuén was in every way as dedicated as Father Serra and even more capable. For thirty-four years the destinies of the California missions were guided by these two spiritual giants.

Within half a century, the New World representatives of the Spanish king had planted a chain of twenty missions on the California coast, counting Santa Inés (1804) and San Rafael Arcangel (1817), built after Lasuén's death. The Mexican government was to add the twenty-first before the end of the mission era.

The padres had come to convert the Indians, and for the thousands they induced to come into the missions this meant a drastic change from their age-old way of life. Innately individualistic, the Indians resented and occasionally resisted the highly organized life of the missions. Consequently, conversions went slowly at first. The padres persisted.

Were the missions good or bad for the Indians? Some claim that the mission system was nothing but a thinly disguised form of slavery, despite its religious aspect. The Indians received food and shelter but no wages for compulsory labor and regimentation. The training in crafts and trades that the Indians received, the critics said, was superficial.

The mission fathers separated the male and female Indians, broke up ancient life patterns, weaned the Indians away from their native skills in living off the land. When the missions were secularized and the Indians were left suddenly to their own devices, they perished.

San Diego de Alcalá

Scarcely two weeks after sighting San Diego Bay in 1769, Father Serra began building the first mission in Alta California. It was dedicated to St. Didacus of Alcalá, who died in Spain in 1463 much revered for his miracles. The mission was a crude affair of brush, in what is now Old

Town, San Diego. In 1774, when Father Serra was in Carmel, the mission was moved six miles up Mission Valley from Old Town.

A large church was built, and to this were later added a house for missionaries, soldiers' quarters, guest rooms, and an infirmary for women. By 1808, San Diego de Alcalá was ready to build a more ambitious church, and in 1813 the building was dedicated. Here, a cross was erected on the spot where the first missionary martyr in California had been murdered. It was the first signpost on El Camino Real, the highway joining the twenty-one missions in California, the four presidios and three pueblos.

With the coming of the Americans, the mission became a barracks for army personnel, and when the troops left, it was turned into a stable. The mission was in ruins for decades until a campaign was started to restore it.

After nearly a century of neglect, this first of the Spanish missions was finally restored and rededicated in 1931. Particularly attractive is the simple façade, with its wide brick steps and outspread walls like welcoming arms. On the left, the handsome *campanario* with its five-niched bell towers rises above the mission gardens. The church interior is gravely unadorned, as was the original. Among the five padres buried here is Father Luis Jayme, martyred by the Indians.

San Luis Rey de Francia

Founded in 1798 by Father Lasuén—his ninth and last mission—San Luis Rey de Francia was a most successful mission. It was named for St. Louis, King of France (1236—1270), the Crusader. By the year 1800 more than a thousand Indian converts inhabited the mission. A French visitor who passed by in 1827 stated that San Luis Rey resembled a glittering white palace, whose buildings covered more than six acres among gardens and orchards. A wide stairway to the orchard looked like the citrus fruit conservatory at Versailles.

The mission did not, however, survive the vicissitudes attributable to the Mexican government's secularization of the missions and the subsequent American occupation. Restoration was started in 1893, however, and the work was done mostly by young seminarians.

The colorful mortuary chapel is one of the most interesting survivals. Octagonal and crowned with a dome, it is graced with an elaborate altarpiece. The church itself is cruciform, with a dome over the crossing, the only dome remaining in the California missions. Visitors admire the gates leading through the thick adobe wall on which were applied designs by Walt Disney artists when they were working on the Zorro films. The sunken gardens and laundry lie spread out in a hollow below the mission and resemble a Roman amphitheater.

The *asistencia* of San Antonio de Pala was built at the foot of Palomar Mountain, some twenty miles from San Luis Rey. An *asistencia* was a sub-mission. The church today is in active use.

San Juan Capistrano

This is the "swallows" mission, and the adobe church, built in 1777 by Father Serra, is California's oldest church still in use. The rest of the structures were built between 1787 and 1810.

This seventh mission, formally founded on November 1, 1776, by Father Serra, fell heir to all the travails so common to California missions at their commencement. Drought, crop failures, disease, and death were common visitors. Despite these obstacles, the mission made great progress, and by 1797 the great stone church, the most magnificent building of the mission era, was begun. It was 146 feet long and twenty-eight feet wide, with a vaulted roof. It took nine years to build and was destroyed in a single day during the earthquake of 1812. Beautiful flowers and flowering vines have overgrown the ruins.

Major restoration of the mission had to wait until the 1920s, when Father St. John O'Sullivan patiently laid out and planted gardens and repaired some of the buildings. Particularly delightful are the gardens, which have become the beauty spot of California. On St. Joseph's Day (March 19), thousands of visitors come to welcome the migrating swallows and see the year-round linnets and mockingbirds.

Of great interest, too, are the crude Indian designs on the ceiling of the nave and the childlike Indian decorations on the Serra Chapel wall, all of which were painted in the bright primary colors so popular with the natives. In contrast is the sophisticated *reredos,* which brings a grand luster to the old adobe chapel. This was brought from Barcelona in 1906 to grace a new cathedral in Los Angeles but, never having been used for that purpose, was installed here during 1922—24. It is thought to be at least three hundred years old.

San Gabriel Arcángel

A tablet at the corner of San Gabriel Boulevard and Lincoln Street near Pico-Rivera, California, commemorates the location of the first Mission San Gabriel. Portolá had camped nearby in 1769, and it was here that the fourth mission was begun, only to be moved five years later to higher ground. California's second civic settlement, the Pueblo de Nuestra Señora la Reina de los Angeles de Porciúncula was founded seven miles away in 1781. Priests from San Gabriel officiated there for a while. In time the Pueblo grew so prosperous that it was known as the Pride of the Missions.

Architecturally, San Gabriel is described as "fortress style," with elements that trace back to the cathedral at Cordova, with its capped buttresses, long, narrow windows, and arched shell decorations above the doors.

The church has been preserved with all its strong colors—red, gold, and green. The painted wooden ceiling conceals the original beams. Here, too, are some remarkable paintings made by Indians. And the bells of San Gabriel toll above the sounds of motor cars.

San Fernando Rey de España

The mission is twenty-three miles from the Plaza of Los Angeles. Not far away, gold was discovered and the first oil well in California drilled. This seventeenth mission was founded by Father Lasuén in 1797. The growing population soon outstripped the facilities of the first church built in 1797, and a second and then a third church were built. The discovery of gold nearby brought fortune hunters and squatters. By 1847, the Americans had taken possession of the mission.

Decay had already set in. By 1896, writers were lamenting the deterioration of the mission, but in the 1950s much of the restoration of San Fernando was completed.

The church of San Fernando Mission re-created the atmosphere of the original. Wherever possible, Indian designs have been reproduced where they are still traceable; where they had become obliterated, new decorations were introduced that were copied from other missions. There is also a wealth of architectural detail. Big hand-hewn doors, graced with mission-made locks and a snakelike river-of-life pattern, welcome visitors to the *convento*. Shell patterns above the doors are ancient motifs.

Visitors may see the wine cellar, the Moorish windows, the portable altar, and the murals. A star-shaped fountain stands near the House of the Fathers, and across the street in the park is a statue of Father Serra.

San Buenaventura

The ninth mission had been planned by the Inspector-General of Mexico, Don José de Galvez, and was founded on March 31, 1782, by Father Serra in today's town of Ventura, just sixty-one miles from Los Angeles by way of El Camino Real. By the early nineteenth century, San Buenaventura was a thriving mission. All missions suffered under the Mexican administration that followed the territory's independence from Spain, but San Buenaventura suffered somewhat less than her unfortunate sisters.

The cream-textured façade of the mission church with its red trim has changed little since it was rebuilt in 1812, although the church interior was authentically restored in 1957. Many interesting features remain. The church altar is more than a hundred years old. A statue of the Immaculate Conception was brought from the Philippines in 1801. The baptistry has the original font, and pictures of the Stations of the Cross are just the way they were in 1809. The massive tower on the right of the building has old bells dating back to 1781 and 1825. Two of the mission's original olive trees still stand on this picturesque site.

Santa Bárbara

Father Serra thought that the site of the future Santa Bárbara, the Queen of the Missions, was an earthly paradise. He did not, however, live to see the establishing of the mission; the honor fell to Father Lasuén, who dedicated the tenth mission in 1786.

In its 175-year history, Santa Bárbara has seen Indian wars, Mexican battles, bandit raids, fires, and earthquakes. On June 29, 1925, an earthquake toppled the towers of the church. The temblor opened gaps in the roof, and buttresses were torn from the walls. It took almost two years to restore the church and to retouch the Indian paintings. The present church is 165 feet long, thirty-nine feet wide, and thirty feet high. Thirteen romanesque arches support the façade. The fathers' living quarters are in an adobe building 240 feet long and fifty feet wide. Some sixty Franciscans are housed here. The Sacred Garden at the rear of the church can be seen from the western tower. This unique and lovely garden is one of Californa's proudest ornaments.

The altar light at Santa Bárbara has been kept burning for more than a hundred years. At the mission museum you will see the first altar, the first music studied by the Indians, parchment volumes of prayers, Serra's vestments, and other treasures. In the east garden cemetery is the dust of thousands of Indian converts as well as that of Don José Ortega, the discoverer of San Francisco Bay.

Santa Inés

The last southern mission to be founded is forty-five miles northwest of Santa Bárbara. Built toward the end of the mission-building days in 1804, it completed the chain between San Diego and San Francisco. It was situated in the heart of Indian country, and its history is full of romantic tales. One recounts how an Indian girl ran all the way over the mountains to warn the mission fathers of an imminent Indian attack, only to die of exhaustion shortly thereafter. She lies buried in the mission's church walls.

Today a lovely *campanario* rises above the little graveyard, where sixteen hundred Indians are buried. The present façade of the mission is less than half the width of the original, which extended south for twenty-four arches. The church has been restored and repainted and still looks just the way it must have to the Indian worshipers in 1817. The paintings of the martyrdom of Santa Inés (Saint Agnes) also appear to have been painted by Indians. A large painting of a Nativity, found in a mission outbuilding, is ascribed by some to Murillo, the Spanish Renaissance painter.

La Purísima Concepción

The full name of the mission is "La Misión de la Purísima Concepción de la Santísima Virgen María, Madre de Dios y Nuestra Señora" (The Mission of the most Immaculate Conception of the Most Holy Virgin Mary, Mother of God and Our Lady). Originally founded in the present city of Lompoc on December 8, 1787, by Father Lasuén, it was moved to its present site, four miles east of Lompoc, after an earthquake in 1812. Some ruins of the first mission can still be seen in the center of the town.

When restoration began in the 1930s only a few pitiful fragments of walls and a few lonely pillars remained. Today, the mission is more completely restored than any other and is in fact the largest and most complete historic restoration in the West. The work was done by youths of the Civilian Conservation Corps, who closely approximated in skill the Indian craftsmen of 120 years previous.

La Purísima offers the visitor one of those truly rare opportunities of seeing how the Indians practiced the mission crafts, such as the processing of hides, the preparation of candles, the sawing of beams.

The restoration catches the straightforward simplicity of the mission atmosphere with furnishings copied from other missions; rough-textured walls and floors and crude wall decorations. There are no benches in the church, for it was the common practice in Spanish and Mexican churches for the congregation to sit or kneel on the floor. The mission is now a state park.

San Luis Obispo de Tolosa

The fifth mission to be established in California is in the heart of the city of San Luis Obispo. Father Serra dedicated it in 1772. After a period of comparative prosperity and growth, decay set in. Earthquakes shattered the mission church, crops were ruined through neglect, and flocks were sharply reduced. Valued at $70,000 in 1834, it was bought for $510 at public auction in 1845.

Today restoration and new buildings have joined to make the mission one of the more imposing historic and religious showplaces in the state. At the entrance to the church are doors from olden days with ancient hinges and interesting panels. An original statue of St. Luis hangs over the altar. The ceiling is ornamented with blue stars that shine almost as brightly as the day they were painted there by Indians.

San Miguel Arcangel

The sixteenth mission in the series was dedicated to Saint Michael and is situated in what is today the extreme northern part of San Luis Obispo County, nine miles north of Paso Robles and directly on El Camino Real. Father Lasuén blessed the place in 1797.

Trials and tribulations were not long in coming. The church bell cracked, the crops were destroyed, some of the fathers were poisoned by Indians. Despite a growing prosperity, death and violence continued to haunt the mission, and by 1841 there were only thirty Indians, whereas twelve hundred had lived there in 1804.

Restoration has done wonders for the mission, much of it carried out by the Franciscan fathers. Among the more interesting sights are the Munras murals, as vivid today as they were 117 years ago; the octagonal multicolored pulpit that hangs on the right wall, a wishing chair in the sanctuary, and a large shell in shades of pink and green back of the pulpit.

San Antonio de Padua

The third mission founded by Father Serra, in 1771, is today one of the most interesting ones. It has been faithfully restored to an authentic approximation of its original state. A delightful *campanario* stands unique among the bell walls of the mission chain. Behind it lies a barrel vault that leads into the church itself.

The restored interior of the church is pleasantly subdued in decoration All the statues are originals; some were kept by the Indians during the years when the mission was neglected. A beamed-ceiling structure is unique in the mission chain. Of interest to music lovers is a display of devices in the museum by which the padres taught music to the Indians.

The loveliness of San Antonio's natural setting is very much apparent today. Bare hills rise behind the mission but nearby are great oak forests. The buildings are surrounded by carpets of spring wild flowers. All this is decidedly in contrast with many missions, which no longer retain their original bucolic atmosphere, situated as they are in cramped urban settings.

14

Nuestra Senora de Soledad

Our Lady of Solitude Mission was founded on October 9, 1791, by Father Lasuén one mile west of the present Highway 101 and three miles south of the town of Soledad, on a brown and barren plain in what is today Monterey County. From the beginning the mission had little luck, and it deteriorated. Until 1954, it was still in ruins. Restoration is beginning to give Soledad much of its original appearance. The chapel and padres' wing have been completed under the auspices of the Native Daughters of the Golden West.

San Carlos Borromeo de Carmelo

The second mission was founded on Monterey Bay on June 3, 1770, by Father Serra. The following year it was moved a few miles south to the sunny little valley where the playful Carmel River joins the Pacific Ocean. Father Serra lived there until his death in 1784.

The exact site of the original church erected at Carmel is unknown, but it was within a hundred yards of the present church building. A second church was built nine years after Serra's death, and a third probably around the second building. The star window of the present church is unique in California mission buildings and was probably inspired by the architectural ideas of Father Lasuén, who was also responsible for the column arches and the distinctive Moorish tower.

In 1856, long before Carmel became the famous literary center it is today, Father Sorentine of Monterey discovered the graves of Fathers Serra, Lasuén, and other Franciscan missionaries and marked them. In 1882, Father Casanova cleared the place and began restoring the Carmel mission. The restoration work was abandoned, not to be resumed until the 1930s. It was completed in the 1950s, and even Father Serra's minuscule cell was carefully rebuilt.

In its superb setting against the sea and mountains, Carmel Mission is the romantic beauty of the California chain. The restored church is equally beautiful in its quiet, almost unadorned simplicity. The present reredos, built in 1957, is adapted from the one at the Mission Dolores. In the mortuary chapel stands the treasured statue of the Virgin that traveled with Father Serra to the founding of the San Diego Mission.

San Juan Bautista

The fifteenth of the California missions was founded in 1797 by Father Lasuén. A series of Indian raids followed in which many converted Indians were massacred. Suppression of these revolts came quickly and mercilessly in spite of Father Lasuén's constant intervention on behalf of the wayward Indians. There is still at the mission a singular barrel organ that was used during an Indian raid to stun the attackers with its lively melodies. The bandits Joaquín Murieta and Tiburcio Vasquez were frequent visitors here.

To visit San Juan Bautista today is to step back in time almost 150 years, for the mellowed old building stands adjacent to a state park and among houses and shops dating from late mission days.

Santa Clara de Asís

This mission lies in the city of Santa Clara, forty-two miles south of San Francisco and four miles from the city of San José. It was the eighth mission to be founded. The year was 1777. From the first, the Santa Clara Valley was a garden spot, and it was here that the first nurseries were constructed. The pueblo of San José, a few miles distant, was the first state capital and the cradle of California education.

The richly ornamented façade of Santa Clara Mission church is a modern intepretation of the simple structure of 1825. The interior, however, has embellishments of a Victorian cast that detract from the original atmosphere. Whereas in most of the missions the decorations were designed and painted by amateurs, the ceiling of Santa Clara was painted by a professional, Augustín Dávila, who was imported from Mexico to do this work.

The mission gardens are among California's loveliest. Olive trees planted in 1822 are still flourishing. There is an original Castilian rose bush, and in the cruciform grape arbor is the oldest grape vine in Northern California.

Santa Cruz

The twelfth mission lies on Mission Hill in the city of Santa Cruz. Father Lasuén blessed the spot in 1791, and the cornerstone of the church was laid in 1793. It was the least prosperous of all the California missions; by 1842, floods, earthquakes and general neglect had ravaged the mission to such an extent that its value was put at less than $1000.

Few of the original mission buildings remain. A replica of the old mission church was built in 1931, and to lovers of California lore these precincts are a great delight. The church contains the statues, paintings, and tabernacle used when the mission was active. The tiny chapel, rosy with light from tinted windows, is used for weddings and private masses.

San José de Guadalupe

The fourteenth mission to be created was probably the most daring. The district was wild, the Indians were hostile. Father Lasuén selected the site, and in 1797 the usual foundation ceremonies were held. In Gold Rush days the mission was converted into a trading post.

Of the large complex of buildings that once stood here, only a remnant of a building remains. This structure now serves as a museum and chapel. Noteworthy exhibits in the museum are the original baptismal font, vestments of the early priests, and some fine Mexican statues.

San Francisco de Asís (Mission Dolores)

Although three missions had already been founded in the northern part of Upper California, Father Serra pressed for one to be dedicated to St. Francis of Assisi. "If St. Francis desires a mission, let him show us his port," said the Inspector-General. In 1769, Portolá stumbled upon

Golden Gate Bridge and San Francisco

Near and far shapes have a peculiar clarity in the typical San Francisco fog, which obscures the middle distance in this photo taken from the high vantage point of Marin County. Farthest away, but distinct, is the upthrusting skyline of Baghdad-by-the-Bay, San Francisco, the heart of Northern California.

NORTHERN CALIFORNIA

Mariposa Grove: Giant Sequoias

These giant trees, typical of California, grow to heights of 250 to 300 feet. They thrive at elevations of from 4,500 to 8,000 feet in the Sierra Nevada. Mariposa Grove is near the southern (Fresno) entrance to Yosemite. About 190 of the trees here have a trunk diameter of over 10 feet.

Sacramento: The Capitol Building

Sacramento is the state capital of California. Founded shortly before the gold rush of 1849, it became the supply center for the gold mines in the neighborhood and, soon after 1854, the state capital. The Capitol Building, designed by F. M. Butler in Roman Classic architectural style, was started in 1861 and finished in 1874. The top of its golden dome is 237 feet above ground level. A beautiful 40-acre park, with more than 1000 varieties of rare trees and shrubs, surrounds it.

Mount Shasta

Rising to a height of 14,163 feet in the most northern part of California, Mount Shasta is the most picturesque mountain in the state. Once a volcano, the mountain now has five glaciers on its slopes, and it towers above the city of Mt. Shasta.

Sutter's Fort, Sacramento

Built in 1839, Sutter's Fort was the first outpost of white men in the interior of California. Captain John August Sutter, a Swiss ex-army officer, took up a 50,000-acre grant by swearing allegiance to Mexico and named it New Helvetia in honor of his old country. There he built the fort as his castle, with twelve guns mounted on the ramparts. He started a lively trade and raised cattle, and in 1848 the town of Sacramento was laid out and founded on Sutter's farm grounds. In that year one of his carpenters, James W. Marshall, found gold near Coloma while con-

structing a mill for Sutter. The gold rush that ensued overran his fort and property and destroyed his farm. His cattle were stolen and ruined. He moved to Pennsylvania and died in 1880 in Washington, D.C. The fort still stands, now restored, on the original site.

San Francisco de Asís (Mission Dolores) Mission Church, San Francisco

This mission is famous all over the world because it gave its name to one of America's greatest cities. The old mission, and especially the church, look almost the same as when they were completed in 1791. The style of the church combines Mission-Corinthian and Moorish motifs. The redwood roof is still tied together with rawhide. The original bells still toll in the belltower. When the lusty city broke out in flames during the big earthquake of 1906, the mission remained untouched by the violent upheaval.

San Carlos Borromeo del Rio Carmelo (Carmel Mission) Entrance and Mission Church

The mission is the living heart of the Catholic population of Carmel but is also the pride of the whole artistic community. People of all faiths contributed to its restoration, to make it the most beautiful of all. It retains the atmosphere of yesterday; huge wooden gates separate it from the hustle and bustle of modern life. Romantic flower gardens frame the unusual Moorish architecture of the stone church, where Fathers Junípero Serra, Fermín Lasuén, Juan Crespi, and Julián Lopez are buried. Harry W. Downie, an authority on mission architecture, and Father Michael D. O'Connell, pastor of the mission church since 1933, are mainly responsible for the reconstruction of this outstanding historical landmark of California.

San Francisco: Old Cemetery (Mission Dolores)

The romantic cemetery adjoining the mission church is most interesting, and the inscriptions on the gravestones tell quite a story. Buried here are Indians, Spanish captains, victims of vigilantes, Irish-Americans, and Spanish and Mexican civil officials.

High walls surround the rather narrow grounds separating this highly historic location from busy Dolores Street, which it faces. Only the high tower of the Dolores basilica next door looks out from this tranquil enclosure.

Yosemite Valley from Inspiration Point

Emerging from the dark Wawona Tunnel at just about this point, the visitor inevitably has a sense of gazing back into endless time as he looks down into the fabulous Yosemite Valley. The hazy, verdant fusion of air, light, and water is dominated by El Capitan. Far in the background rises the inimitable Half Dome and the abrupt prominence of Clouds Rest, and closer by is Sentinel Dome, guarding the Cathedral Rocks, which hover over the romantic Bridal Veil Falls.

Scene at the Merced River, Yosemite Valley

As one looks eastward in the deep valley, the slowly flowing Merced River widens in the distance beneath the great Yosemite Falls. In the background is Lost Arrow, with Yosemite Point behind it. The name Lost Arrow derives from a legend of the Ahwahnee Indians, who once lived in the valley.

Yosemite National Park: Vernal Falls

Yan-O-Pah was the Indian name for the steady mist and beneficent spray that emanated from the very heavy Vernal Falls pictured here. This is the Merced River, a white wall descending more than 315 feet into the verdant valley below.

Tuolumne Meadows

Here, for the twentieth-century collector of scenery, is the magnificent eastern approach to Yosemite National Park via Tioga Pass, 9,941 feet in elevation. Across the mirror-still lake are the high snow-capped mountains of Cathedral and Johnson Peaks. In late spring and early summer, carpets of simple flowers are everywhere —buttercup, blue-bell, and many others.

Midway Point, Monterey Peninsula
The rock of Midway Point, with its lone cypress, is perhaps the most often photographed spot in California. Situated on Seventeen Mile Drive, famous for its scenic views, Midway Point shows up against the background of the Santa Lucia Mountains.

Monterey: Historic Colton Hall

The Constitutional Convention of the state of California, which drew up the state's first constitution, met here from September 1 to October 15, 1849. Colton Hall was built in 1847—1848 by Walter Colton, a Navy chaplain and the first American alcalde—mayor—in the Mexican period. Monterey was the capital of Alta California under Spanish and Mexican rule.

Picturesque Beach at Pacific Grove

Cliffs and beautiful sand beaches are typical along the world-famous Seventeen Mile Drive, which follows the coast between Pacific Grove and Carmel. Looking closely at the picture, you will see in the foreground a sandy beach close to the colorful rocks and foaming waves, and just behind, people swimming in the quiet, deep-blue waters of the Pacific Ocean.

San Juan Bautista: Façade of Mission Church

To visit this interesting mission is an experience. The whole town of San Juan Bautista, particularly the buildings on the plaza facing the mission, is kept as it was a hundred years ago.

Fishing Fleet, Monterey

Monterey has a lot of old-world atmosphere. Fish canneries and fishing have been Monterey's main industries. The professional fishermen are mostly Italians, but there are also quite a few Portuguese, Chinese, and Japanese families in this business. Fisherman's Wharf is a colorful picture on the waterfront of Monterey.

Carmel:
Mission San Carlos Borromeo

Carmel-by-the-Sea is the famous art center of the Monterey Peninsula.

Close to the "Village" is the famous *Mission San Carlos Borromeo del Rio Carmelo*, which gave the city its name. Restored completely by devoted local craftsmen and well-to-do sponsors, it influences the whole appearance of Carmel. Three Carmelite monks were the first to visit this site in 1602, landing on the cypress-covered slopes of Carmel Bay. This reminded them so much of Mt. Carmel in Palestine that they named it after that site in the Holy Land. Junípero Serra, father of California missions, later founded the mission in 1770. He died and was buried here in 1784.

Oakland:
Dockside at Lake Merritt

Just across San Francisco's Bay Bridge, Oakland's Lake Merritt is a delightful haven for local sailing enthusiasts. Lake Merritt is the only tidal lake in the heart of a California city.

Palo Alto: Stanford University

Just a few miles south of San Francisco is the city of Palo Alto, with its famous Stanford University, established as a memorial to their son by Senator and Mrs. Leland Stanford in 1885. Occupying 8,800 acres, this is one of the finest universities in the country. The $22,000,000 Medical School covers 60 acres and includes school, professional hospital, and library. Hoover Memorial Tower (background) houses one of the country's most extensive collections of documents of World Wars I and II.

The Pacific Coast

Along the Great Highway (Skyline Boulevard) and, farther south, the Coast Highway to Pedro Point and Devil's Slide, San Francisco's Pacific coastline offers a magnificent variety of beautiful beaches, dramatic rock formations, vivid flowers, and vines. At the northwest corner of the city are the offshore Seal Rocks, favorite resting place of a large colony of sea lions, and a perennially favorite view.

Berkeley:
University of California

Here is shown the campanile of one of America's most important and most controversial universities. Attracting students from all over the world, the University of California spreads its durable and stately architecture over many valuable acres, and echoes to the sound of many tongues, a short drive from San Francisco over the Bay Bridge.

San Francisco from Yerba Buena Island

Eight miles long, the San Francisco-Oakland Bay Bridge is a fascinating drive for tourists. This view from Yerba Buena (the early name for San Francisco) shows the city partially shrouded by typical, and temporary, fog.

Byways of the City of San Francisco

Native San Franciscans insist that their city offers much more than meets the tourist's eye. Here, one of the city's charming cul de sacs, a little alley, offers a meditative shopper the romantic side of a busy metropolis.

Fisherman's Wharf, San Francisco

Hundreds of fishing boats and the city's commercial fishing fleets dock here. Fisherman's Wharf is an outstanding attraction for tourists and natives alike, its rugged and colorful atmosphere providing the setting for some of the world's most famous seafood restaurants. Familiar names among gourmets, some of the more illustrious establishments are Fisherman's Grotto, Alioto's, Sabella, Tarantino's, Arturo's, DiMaggio's, Castagnola, and the Franciscan Restaurant.

City Hall and Civic Center, San Francisco

Cascading fountains and a tremendous shallow pool mark the approach to San Francisco's Civic Center. Ten whole blocks of public edifices surround this area, which is dominated by City Hall, a granite building with a magnificent dome, French Renaissance in style. Included in the vast area devoted to public interest is the Civic Auditorium, seating nearly 10,000, the city-owned San Francisco Opera House, Brooks Hall (convention site), the State Building, the main branch of the San Francisco Public Library, and the Veteran's War Memorial Building, which houses the San Francisco Museum of Art.

Telegraph Hill—Coit Tower,
San Francisco

A hill with an astounding variety of names, Loma Alta became Telegraph Hill during the Civil War. In the mid 1800's, Chileans and their goats preempted the foothills, the Irish taking over the summits later until the Italians poured in and won the hill for keeps in the 1890's. Today, Telegraph Hill is the home of various "upper bohemian" dwellings, the tenants holding tightly to their demi-monde classification.

Nob Hill, San Francisco

Here, B.E.Q. (Before Earthquake), many of San Francisco's and the nation's most important people were neighbors: Charles Crocker, Senator George Hearst, Mark Hopkins, Collis P. Huntington, Lloyd Tevis, James A. Fair, Leland Stanford. Their palaces and mansions were destroyed by the 1906 earthquake, but some of the illustrious names live on in the Mark Hopkins and Fairmont Hotels, Stanford Apartments, and Huntington Park.

Church of Sts. Peter and Paul, San Francisco

Slender, delicate spires soaring skyward, the most beautiful Roman Catholic Church in San Francisco stands in Washington Square, easily visible throughout all the city. Its sonorous chimes are heard downtown.

Golden Gate Park, San Francisco
Japanese Tea Garden

Golden Gate Park (four miles long and half a mile wide) encompasses the Tea Garden, which is wonderfully landscaped in oriental design and includes a temple, a granite shrine, reflecting pools, and an arched bridge. Within these delightful acres are other gardens, lakes, playgrounds, and groves, as well as the Morrison Planetarium, the Steinhart Aquarium, the California Academy of Sciences, the Conservatory, and the De Young Museum, which houses San Francisco's largest fine arts collection.

San Francisco Maritime State Park

History comes alive with a visit to San Francisco's floating museum of ancient sailing ships. The two pictured here rest at the foot of celebrated Hyde Street.

Goethe and Schiller Monument, San Francisco

San Francisco's Golden Gate Park pays homage with fine statuary to Germany's most illustrious poets.

Washington Square and Russian Hill, San Francisco

Towering new apartment buildings, elegant homes with private gardens predominate in this distant view of fashionable Russian Hill, which overlooks San Francisco Bay and is the subject of speculation as to its name. Educated guesswork assigns it to the fact that the graves of several supposedly Russian sailors are located here in the vicinity of prominent Vallejo Street.

Lombard Street, Most Crooked Street in San Francisco

Winding down from Russian Hill, Lombard Street protects breakneck drivers from sudden disastrous descent with cleverly plotted and beautifully planted flower garden beds. Zigging and zagging as they must to travel this most precipitous street, drivers enjoy an intimate glimpse of San Francisco's most unusual small community, with its attractive apartment houses and private homes.

Union Square in Downtown San Francisco

Within the shadows of the old St. Francis Hotel, historical Union Square presents a palm-shaded approach to the city's most famous shopping district. Beneath the broad acres of Union Square is one of the nation's largest underground garages—a parking lot that accommodates 1700 automobiles.

Chinatown, San Francisco

San Francisco's large Chinese population lives very much in modern American style, but the oriental flavor of Chinatown is retained in typical Chinese architecture, decorative design in roof lines and lighting fixtures, and the merchandise offered in stores and shops. A delightful fragrance emanates from the kitchens of Chinatown's many excellent restaurants, to which tourists and local people are attracted by the promise of exotic foods.

Cable Car on Hyde Street, San Francisco

A treasured holdover from 1873, the city's creaking cable cars are kept in top condition by a San Francisco devoted to its earlier and most cherished mode of travel. These antiquated vehicles, reminders of a reckless youth, are well-preserved mementos of the past. And Alcatraz, notorious penitentiary of that era, continues now in paradoxical San Franciscan fashion as a coming "monument to peace," with Marin County's hills providing a background.

Golden Gate Bridge

Aside from being one of the most beautiful bridges in the world, this is one of the longest single span suspension bridges. Spanning the Golden Gate, it connects San Francisco with Marin County. Golden Gate Bridge runs its 4,200-foot length between two huge towers, each over 70 stories high, tallest and largest in the world. Carrying a six-lane highway and two pedestrian walks, the bridge soars 242 feet above San Francisco Bay, shown here with old Fort Baker to the extreme right.

Beach near San Francisco

One of San Francisco's many marvelous natural beaches. Numerous small, hidden coves delight the free-roving, modern explorer of this fabulous peninsula, which offers fine surfing, swimming, and boating against a dramatic background of rockbound cliffs and flowering hillsides.

Lassen Peak
(Lassen Volcanic National Park)

Lassen Peak, the highest point (10,456 feet) in this National Park, is an active volcano with continuous eruptions as recent as 1914 to 1921. The park is full of smaller volcanos, fumaroles, hot springs, lava fields, cinder cones, mud volcanos, and boiling lakes and pots. This highly interesting National Park in northeastern California can be reached and traversed on good roads from Red Bluff, Chester, or Susanville.

Shasta Dam and Lake Shasta
Just eight miles north of Redding rises Shasta Dam, 602 feet above its foundation and 3,500 feet long, holding back the waters of Lake Shasta. On very clear days, the snow-covered Mount Shasta is visible in the far background.

Grazing Deer

In the mountains of California, deer, bear, elk, chipmunk, beaver, porcupine, squirrel, and bird extend to man a trusting welcome into their home.

Burney Falls

Dropping down in several streams over a 134-foot-high lava wall, Burney Falls is the main attraction of McArthur-Burney Falls State Park, in the eastern part of Northern California. There are campsites in the park, and Lake Britton, with boating, swimming, and good bass fishing, is adjacent.

The Great Forests of Yosemite and Meadows in the Sierra Nevada

Many forests grow from the valley floors to the heights of the surrounding mountains. The giant sequoias are found in several locations. Ponderosa and Jeffrey Pines are profuse, the latter made durably famous by the ancient specimen atop Sentinel Dome and throughout the forests, where there are also many varieties of coniferous trees, notably the Hemlock and Sierra Juniper. The Pine family is well represented by the Sugar, Digger, Knobcone, Whitebark, Lodgepole, and Western White; and there are the White, Red, and Douglas Firs and the distinctive single-leaf Piñons.

Lake Tahoe

This beautiful mountain lake in the Sierra Nevada, at an altitude of 6,225 feet, is 21.6 miles long and 12 miles wide, with a surface area of 194 square miles. The deepest lake in the United States, it is surrounded by mountains just over 10,000 feet in altitude. Its water is clear and deep blue. It is a favorite vacation spot, and attractive resorts crowd the shores of the lake.

Yosemite Valley from Glacier Point

A heart-thumping view from the promontory of Glacier Point. Here, only a small part of the tremendous panorama can be shown, but beyond the frame of this picture there is the living beauty of the meadows, the forests, and the primeval rocks. Visible are Yosemite Falls, the valley, the Merced River, and the modern roads.

*Half Dome,
Yosemite National Park*

One of the most unusual "rocks" to be found on our planet. The western face of Half Dome was once sheared completely away, as if by a giant spoon. The black "face" seen here is an almost concave depression in the vertical façade, visible from nearly every point in and around the valley.

El Capitan, Yosemite Valley

The sheer and forbidding profile of a mighty mountain, the largest single block of solid granite in the world, elevation 7,569 feet.

On Sentinel Dome (Yosemite National Park)

An old twisted Jeffrey Pine grows from the rocks of this famous outlook, framing a beautiful view of other peaks in this great mountainous region.

Auto Road through Wawona Tree, Mariposa Grove

The very biggest of all the giant sequoias accommodated a tunnel built for the auto road in Mariposa Grove. It was called the Wawona Tree (Indian name for big tree). The tunnel, an attestation to its measurements, was eight feet wide, ten feet high, and twenty-six feet long. It fell in the winter of 1969.

San Juan Bautista: Mission Gardens

This beautiful garden is well worth a visit. It is kept up by people with a fine understanding of tradition and with artistic sense. The picture shows a small side gate leading to the church, framed by two old grape vines; an old apple tree is in the foreground.

The Blooming Coast of Monterey Peninsula

Monterey Peninsula, with its interesting shoreline of reefs and rocks and intermittent sandy beaches, has a charm of its own. An added attraction is the many flowers, especially the blossoms of the ice plant, growing in abundance along the northern coast of the peninsula. They are in the foreground of the picture, which shows in the background Pacific Grove, one of the romantic villages on beautiful Seventeen Mile Drive, which follows the coast of the peninsula to Pebble Beach and Carmel.

November Day on Lake Tahoe

This picture of the beautiful mountain lake was taken on a dark November day just before a heavy snowfall, which covered the mountains and valleys. The area around Lake Tahoe is famous for winter sports activities. Eight miles west is Squaw Valley, site of the Winter Olympics of 1960.

Sunset at Cypress Point

Sunsets on the Pacific coast are unforgettable. From the deepest red to brilliant yellow, orange, and green, the colors of the sky change from minute to minute. This picture, taken at Cypress Point near Pebble Beach, shows the silhouette of a Monterey cypress (*Cypressus macrocarpa*), native only to Cypress Point and the surrounding Monterey Peninsula. It grows naturally nowhere else.

the Golden Gate and on October 9, 1776, the Mission of San Francisco was born. By 1823, it was popularly called Dolores to distinguish it from San Francisco Solano to the north.

The little church of Mission Dolores looks almost the way it did when it was completed in 1791. The original bells hang from rawhide thongs in the bell tower and are rung on special occasions. The long, narrow chapel has changed little since the day when Indians knelt on its tile floors. Noteworthy is the baroque reredos, a fine example of Mexican ecclesiastical art. Mission Indians painted the lovely decorations.

The overwhelming mass of the Mission Dolores basilica dwarfs the neighboring mission chapel and its little woodsy cemetery, but the picture in its ensemble is one of peace and tranquility.

San Rafael Arcángel

The next-to-last mission, San Rafael, fifteen miles north of San Francisco, was dedicated in 1817 and was intended as a place where the Indians might recuperate from their illnesses. The original mission was razed in the 1870s, but a replica of the old chapel now stands in its place. It has a star window copied from the one at Carmel Mission. The interior of the chapel is built on modern lines, with some concessions to mission style in the arched sanctuary and the deep-set windows.

San Francisco Solano

The last of California's missions is the farthest north, in the city of Sonoma, thirty miles north of San Francisco. It was started in 1823 by Father José Altimira, a young and energetic native of Barcelona.

The mission chapel was completely restored by the state of California during 1911—13 to approximate the look it had in 1840, when it was erected to serve as the parish chapel for the town of Sonoma. A traditional arcade crosses the front of the old monastery wing, which is the oldest portion of the mission and the oldest building in Sonoma (1825). The restored chapel's interior is being carefully furnished to approximate the mission era.

Spain in California

Small towns began to grow around the missions and near the presidios under military rule. The pueblo of Los Angeles, founded by Spain in 1781, was settled by colonists from Mexican Sinaloa. Its first name was El Pueblo de Nuestra Señora la Reina de los Angeles de Porciúncula (The Village of Our Lady, Queen of Angels). The original Indian inhabitants of the area were dominated by a tribe of the Gabrielino Indians, a peaceful and self-disciplined group, and by the Shoshoneans, who maintained twenty-eight villages in what is now Los Angeles County. Their principal village was Yang-na.

The first settlers of San Francisco came from Sonoma and Tubac in Mexico in 1776. The 240 immigrants came over the High Sierra in the preceding winter. One woman died and eight children were born on that trek.

So weak was Spain's power in California that Russian fur traders were not resisted when they built a stockade, Fort Ross, north of San Francisco in 1812. United States, British, French, and South American ships were treated respectfully in California harbors, though they were not supposed to enter them.

Mexico in California

After Mexico won independence from Spain in 1821, the Indians occasionally revolted, most strongly in 1824. Their cause was taken up by a party of progressive Castilians and in 1834 Mexico ordered the friars of the missions to confine themselves to religion. Mission lands were to be distributed to the Indian converts and to other colonists, "Californios." The colonists got all the lands and cattle, and the little cash that the Indians received went quickly.

Generous land grants were given to Spanish colonists, who built ranchos of adobe brick, surrounded by vast pasture lands for cattle. They were hospitable to strangers, though they worked the Indians as peons.

On April 9, 1822, Governor Pablo Vicente de Sola and ten delegates—eight military officers and two priests—met at Monterey and proclaimed California independent of Spain and dependent alone on the Empire of Mexico. In the same year the province set up a legislative body. Indians were declared free citizens, ports were opened to trade, import and export duties and taxes on crops were levied, a military force was formed, and courts were created. California was a territory of the Republic of Mexico until 1846. The rancheros led lives of leisure, varied by an occasional revolt such as that of 1836, when they proclaimed the "Free and Sovereign State of Alta California." They were generally careful not to shoot at each other and oratory carried the day. Mexico made concessions and they returned to the fold.

COMING OF THE YANKEES

Yankee skippers began to visit California ports late in the eighteenth century, along with trappers and traders. The first ship, the *Otter* of Boston, dropped anchor at Monterey in 1796. The Yankee traders brought supplies to the neglected colonists and carried hides and tallow to Atlantic coast ports. Slowly the American traders acquired land and control of the economy.

Trappers took a fortune in furs from inland parts of the state that the Spaniards had never explored. The towering cliffs, deep canyons, and inspiring back country of Yosemite, about 150 miles east of San Francisco in the rugged heart of the Sierra Nevada mountains, were first described by Captain Joseph R. Walker. He was sent with a party to explore the possibilities of fur trade in the then-unknown Far West in 1833.

The first overland immigrant train reached California in 1841. The Russians at Fort Ross, their outpost on the Northern California coast, sold out to John Augustus Sutter, a Swiss immigrant, in the same year. The trickle of Yankee immigrants swelled. In two years about four thousand Americans made the incredibly difficult overland trip across the Oregon Trail.

MEXICAN WAR

American settlers at Sonoma in Northern California raised the Flag of the Bear on June 14, 1846, and proclaimed an independent California Republic. Though they did not know it, war had begun between the United States and Mexico on May 13. Captain John C. Frémont, a United States topographical engineer, immediately marched to join them with seventy-two mounted riflemen. Captain John D. Sloat sailed into Monterey Bay and raised the American flag on July 7. Two days later the Stars and Stripes were flying over San Francisco and Sonoma.

During the 1840s the New York *Tribune's* Horace Greeley was advising young men to turn their faces to the great West and build up homes and fortunes there. Tales of California as a land of perpetual spring had started the swelling tide of prairie schooners across the land. Immigrants were coming around Cape Horn in 1846. The westering spirit was at work. When war came with Mexico, the Yankees were in control in California.

The skirmishes in California during the war were brief. Mexican Californians surrendered to Captain Frémont's troops near Los Angeles in 1847. On February 2, 1848, California was ceded to the United States by the signing of the Treaty of Guadalupe Hidalgo.

GOLD!

A young New Jersey wagon builder, James Wilson Marshall, made the overland march in 1845 and went to work for Sutter on the land bought from the Russians. There he built a saw mill on the South Fork of the American River, near what is now Coloma. And there, in January of 1848, he picked a few bits of gold out of the sand in the tail race. He was the man who started the greatest mass movement in history, the California Gold Rush. The gold had been discovered nine days before Spain relinquished California.

Soldiers lay down their arms, sailors deserted their ships, farmers abandoned their harvests, and shopkeepers closed shop. By summer time hardly an able-bodied male remained in the young cities of California. Men streamed in from all over the world. The population of the state increased from 15,000 in 1847 to 92,000 in 1850. Veterans of the Mexican War looking for work headed west. In 1849, 549 ships arrived in San Francisco. About half were from the United States, the rest from Europe and the Orient. About 40,000 Forty-niners came by sea. Most were young and male and single. In 1850, more than half of all Californians were in their twenties. The bleaching bones of oxen and mules were strewn beside the Overland Trail.

More than one billion, two hundred million dollars in gold was taken from California hills and streams in the thirty years after 1848. One miner washed $1,500 in gold from a single pan. Men brawled and gambled and spent their money on wild, wild women. In five years the Gold Rush was over. By 1854 the diggings were declining. But unlike almost all other gold rushes in history, this one was the foundation on which great cities and a great state were built. It shaped the West's new style of life. High wages and the gold fever created social freedom, democracy, mobility. Women, who were scarce, were treated with great courtesy. The big fortunes that emerged intact were not those of the miners, largely, but of the merchants, suppliers, bankers, and financiers who used their funds to build railroads.

Though there was no formal law in the mining camps, they policed themselves with a fair degree of justice and democracy. San Francisco, the port town, was the center of lawlessness. The little band of original settlers around Mission San Francisco de Asís named their village Yerba Buena, "good herb" in Spanish, for an aromatic vine that grew profusely thereabouts and was highly prized in cooking. In 1847, by official proclamation, San Francisco became the name of the port city.

In San Francisco, men gambled with their money and their lives. They had practically no city government and not a single police officer. Between December 1849 and June 1851, six great fires all but destroyed the Jewel of the Pacific and burned away many of the gold-wrought fortunes so briefly enjoyed. Five of these terrible fires were clearly incendiary in origin, deliberately caused to cover up the looting of a hysterically stricken city, already nearly paralyzed by lawlessness.

These were days of dedicated vice and uncontrolled gambling. Concomitant sins were protected by unprincipled politicians, and San Francisco became a notorious spawning place for Machiavellian evil of every sort. In 1848, at the end of the Mexican War, a number of ex-soldiers organized themselves into a gang of ruffians known as "The Hounds." Their worst depredations took place in the first seven months of 1849. In July of that year they were driven out of town by Sam Brannan and his "People's Court," forerunner of the first Vigilance Committee.

Another gang, even more odious, who called themselves the "Sydney Ducks," took over where the Hounds left off and were directly responsible for most of the fires in 1849—51. These early gangsters were from England via Sidney, Australia, and it was their unfettered terrorism that brought into being, in 1851, San Francisco's first Vigilance Committee.

Intolerable conditions plagued the city until 1856, when the second Vigilance Committee selected the gamblers and politicians as prime targets. For nearly six years following the drastic actions of the second Vigilance Committee, which included public hangings, the city was comparatively well-behaved, although the notorious Barbary Coast came into being in the early 1860s, in roughly the same area as Sydney Town, the original hangout of the Sydney Ducks. The Barbary Coast flourished until 1914, but except for this red-light reminder of bawdy beginnings, San Francisco's second Vigilance Committee effected needed reforms which gradually removed the taint of infamy, ignorance, and indolence from the city.

INDIAN SKIRMISHES

During the Gold Rush another legendary "man of the hour" appeared in the person of Major James D. Savage. A soldier during the Mexican War, Savage was a trusted friend of the Indians in the San Joaquin area and operated several trading posts in the Mariposa region. With a large force of foothill Indians, he garnered a share of miner's gold. Learning through his Indian wives that a general uprising was imminent, he attempted a stroke of home-spun psychology by capturing a young chief and taking him to San Francisco. When the sights and sounds of the white man's civilization failed in their desired effect, Savage released his unimpressed and contemptuous captive and, admitting defeat, became commanding officer of the Mariposa Battalion.

From 1851 through the spring of 1853, the Mariposa Battalion, charged with the task of controlling Indian activities, alternately distinguished itself or fell into disgrace through the whimsical behavior of Chief Tenaya. Honest but with the wiles of a card-sharp, canny but blunderingly sincere, cautious one day but full of blustering bravado the next, Tenaya led Savage and his six hundred soldiers a mad, bewildering, and frustrating chase among the mountain fastnesses of Yosemite.

For three long years, Tenaya's resistance to the "suggestion" that he comply with the demand that they live on a Fresno River reservation was simple and succinct: "My people do not want anything from the 'Great Father' you tell me about. The Great Spirit is our father, and he has always supplied us with all we need. We do not want anything from white men." The Indians were finally pushed into their mountain retreats by their white "protectors," leaving to the land of their birth only their name, "Yosemitys," the name signifying a full-grown grizzly bear in their language.

CALIFORNIA STATEHOOD

The Gold Rush not only made California famous, it enabled the territory to become a state with unprecedented speed, far ahead of others in the West. The United States acquired California in 1848, but Congress could come to no agreement on its civil government because of the split between slavery and antislavery proponents. For a year, military law, Spanish law, and American law were administered simultaneously in the territory.

In 1849 Brigadier-General Bennet Riley, the military governor, issued a proclamation calling for the formation of a state convention or a plan for a territorial government. On October 10 of that year, forty-eight delegates meeting in convention in Monterey adopted a constitution that was ratified by voters on November 13, 1849. It was the constitution of the State of California until 1879. On the same day Peter H. Burnett was elected governor and John McDougal lieutenant governor; sixteen state senators and thirty-six assemblymen were also elected. The legislature proceeded to elect two United States senators, John C. Frémont and William M. Gwin.

California thereupon became the only state to proclaim itself a state without the permission, through the United States Congress, of the country it was joining. This happened when the military governor resigned, recognizing the new constitution and state government. It took only eight months of wrangling in Congress before California was admitted, on September 9, 1850, as a free state of the Union.

Between 1850 and 1860, the population of the state almost quadrupled, and the federal census counted 379,994 people in California in 1860. Migration had become increasingly diverse. By 1853 one in every ten Californians was Chinese. The Chinese were imported to work while white men hunted for gold. Irishmen came west to build the Central Pacific Railroad. French and Italian immigrants planted vineyards and farmed. Los Angeles attracted Russians and Mexicans.

In this decade, immigrants from New York and New England outnumbered all others, but the state was already becoming remarkably cosmopolitan.

SOUTHERN CALIFORNIA

What of Southern California, while gold and statehood were creating the vast ferment to the north? In the first census made by the Census Bureau in 1850, the county of Los Angeles had 1,610 inhabitants, mostly Mexicans and Indians—and the county comprised 34,000 square miles that stretched from San Diego to Santa Barbara. The people raised cattle, and they joined the boom when the miners' hunger for beef caused cattle prices to soar.

Though fortunes collapsed, banks failed, and unlucky miners drifted all over the state in 1852, new immigrants kept pouring in to homestead on the fabled, fertile acres of Southern California. Often they squatted on ranchos that had never been precisely surveyed or defined. The "Californios" of Spanish descent were frequently the losers in their turn, as the Indians they had dispossessed had been before them. A land commission was finally formed to adjudicate disputes.

A death blow to the ranchos in the Los Angeles area were two years of drought, in 1862 and 1863, that left vast herds of dead carcasses beneath the blazing sun. Scores of the huge Mexican land grants were divided and sold.

THE CIVIL WAR

The mounting storm over slavery tore the controlling Democratic party apart in the 1850s. Southern sympathizers who believed in slavery began overrunning Southern California, with San Bernardino County as their center. Senator David C. Broderick, leader of the antislavery faction, was slain in a duel by a henchman of the slavery faction in 1859. The cry went up for an independent republic on the Pacific. In 1860 Abraham Lincoln carried California by less than a thousand votes. The Republicans controlled the assembly.

California pledged its loyalty to the Union when Fort Sumter fell. California's principal contribution to helping to win the war for the North was gold.

JOHN MUIR

John Muir, born in Scotland in 1838, came with his family as a boy to farm in Wisconsin. After attending the University of Wisconsin he roamed through Canada, walked a thousand miles through the Southern states to the Gulf of Mexico, visited Cuba, and finally settled down in California when he was about thirty, in 1868. A gifted naturalist, Muir contributed accurate and highly respected observations in geology and glaciology. He lived in Yosemite for fifteen years, describing with passionate love the giant Sequoias. To his devotion to conservation we owe the establishment of federal forest reserves (the National Forest system), Yosemite and Sequoia National Parks and, finally, the National Park system.

BOOM AND BUST AGAIN

The first railroad across the Sierra Nevada, the Central Pacific, was completed in May 1869. It brought new multitudes of pioneers and vast corruption. Land titles were clouded, freight rates exorbitant, capital scarce, interest prohibitive in the decade after the Civil War. Wages were low and unemployment high. The people were in an uproar.

The volatile California emotional climate generated a frenzy of speculation in wildcat mining and oil company stocks in the 1860s. An even wilder boom followed—in Nevada silver-mining stocks, sparked by the development of the Comstock Lode's Bonanza mines in 1872. The Gold Rush was sensible in comparison. People all over the state put everything they had or could borrow into stocks. Most of them lost it all. On August 27, 1875, the Bank of California crashed. A severe drought in 1877 intensified the economic depression. From the farms of the interior valleys to the unemployed dock workers, resentment against the powers-that-be smouldered.

Exasperated workingmen were encouraged by artful politicians to vent their wrath on the Chinese, blaming them for all that was wrong. A gang looted the Los Angeles Chinatown, lynching nineteen Chinese. In 1877, Chinese laundries and the docks where Chinese immigrants landed in San Francisco were burned by thousands of rioters. The Workingmen's Party was organized. The people voted against further immigration from China.

At the same time, whether in spite of the hectic pace of change or because of the cosmopolitan ferment, San Francisco by the 1870s had become one of the great cities of the world, one of those rare cities that are stamped with a unique style, elegant and worldly, the style that still enchants their lovers today. Fine mansions, gilded hostelries, first-rate theater, grand opera, and the gaudy dance halls of the Barbary Coast section all contributed to the style.

The political ferment resulted in a new constitution that voters ratified on May 7, 1879. It allowed distinctly more popular control, and the powers of the legislature were curtailed. Among its improvements was the prohibition of convict labor, the institution of the eight-hour working day, and provisions whereby common carriers and corporations could be taxed and controlled and public utilities regulated.

LOS ANGELES AWAKENS AND PARTAKES

The endemic boom-and-bust fever reached Los Angeles in the 1880s, not long after the Southern Pacific and the Santa Fe railroads got there. It was in 1885 that Southern California invented the modern art of high-powered real estate promotion, later exported to Florida. Lyrical descriptions of the garden spot of the world, the marvelous climate, and the resources of the Pacific Coast were broadcast throughout the country. Rate wars between the railroads reduced the fares from Kansas City to Los Angeles to one dollar at one time.

In 1880, there were 11,183 Los Angelenos counted by the census. By 1887 there were more than 70,000. Speculators were wooed by brass bands and barbecues. The golden sun and the fertile soil brought forth a bumper crop of smooth land hucksters. It was not so much fraud as fevered imagination that brought thousands from the East to invest all they had in land. Prices of Los Angeles lots rose from $500 to $5,000 within a year. Towns were laid out that are still unbuilt. Truck gardens rose in price from $350 an acre to $10,000 an acre.

Early in 1888 the fever burnt itself out, for the time being. Prices slid and the paper millionaires were penniless. Bankruptcy abounded. The bubble had burst. Passengers on the trains going east far outnumbered those going west. The hard times that were to afflict the country in the 1890s came early to California. Unemployment was high, bread lines long. Jack London was one of the Californians who joined Coxey's Army in its march on Washington.

Still, in those hard times, some immigrants came west, especially to Southern California. "Change of climate" was a favorite prescription of physicians of the time, and many were the health seekers attracted by California sunshine as a cure for asthma, tuberculosis, and rheumatism. The population of the state had reached more than a million in 1890.

Then came the discovery of oil to bring prosperity to Los Angeles in the 1890s. Surface oil pools had trapped cattle of the early rancheros. Oil had been distilled in small amounts in the 1850s. In the 1880s annual production was up to 690,000 barrels. Then E. L. Doheny and C. A. Canfield sank a shaft with pick, shovel and windlass on ground at Patton and West State Streets in Los Angeles. They had tapped the vast reservoir beneath Los Angeles. By 1900 the state's oil production had risen to 4,319,950 barrels annually.

THE SAN FRANCISCO EARTHQUAKE

At 5:13 A.M. on April 18, 1906, an earthquake shook San Francisco, paused, and then shook again more strongly. The convulsive shudder that traveled the length of the San Andreas fault lasted forty-five seconds. Water mains burst, chimneys toppled, the city gas works exploded, fires broke out in dozens of places and for three full days raged unchecked, ravaging 497 blocks in the heart of the city, causing five hundred million dollars' worth of damage and taking 450 lives. The fires were brought under control at last by dynamiting the magnificent homes on fashionable Van Ness Avenue. Wholesale looting broke out, but was short-lived when martial law was declared with the announcement that any person caught in the commission of a crime was to be shot on sight. Mutual cooperation became the spirit of the day as San Francisco—ignoring those doomsayers who proclaimed she had been punished for her sins—began the monumental task of rebuilding. These people had inherited the spirit of those who made it over the mountains in the prairie schooners, came around Cape Horn in the clipper ships. Never did that spirit shine more brightly. Within three years, despite graft and scandal and political and civic disturbances, 20,000 brand-new buildings had been constructed. In less than a decade, the city celebrated its phoenixlike rise from the ashes with the Panama-Pacific Exposition in 1915, a tremendous carnival that quite firmly reestablished the city's reputation as the glamor capital of the Pacific Coast.

THE PIONEER MOVIEMAKERS

The title of glamor capital was even then being challenged vigorously by Los Angeles. Chicago moviemakers came to sunny Los Angeles in 1907 to finish a rained-out movie, "The Count of

Monte Cristo." The first permanent motion-picture studio was established in 1909. In 1915, half of all American films were being shot in California, and a new and world-wide magic had been created. Hollywood became the mecca for a certain sort of dreamer round the world. By 1927, the moviemakers, cramped by their Wall Street financiers, were in trouble. Along came the talkies to revamp and revitalize the industry. And when next the moviemaking profits ebbed, television arrived.

THE TWENTIETH CENTURY

The spirit of California has continued to be as ebullient in the twentieth century as it was in the nineteenth. The outcry against the Chinese was replaced in the early years of the century with fulminations against the Japanese, imported by large agricultural interests to take the place of the Chinese. Municipal scandal introduced the muck-raking era in California, and a political revolt of liberal Republicans, led by Hiram Johnson, in 1907 came out against domination of the party by "vested interests." The liberal Lincoln-Roosevelt League of the Republicans did result in one of the most comprehensive programs of constructive legislation ever passed in a single session of an American legislature in 1911. The liberals saw no hope within the Republican Party, and they formed the Progressive Party. As a result of the hot feud between the two, California went to the Democrat Woodrow Wilson by the margin of 3,773 votes.

TODAY

Steel mills, aircraft factories, makers of missiles and spacecraft, and electronics manufacturers have remade the economy. Agriculture is still strong. Splendid colleges and universities are occasionally disrupted by a vocal student minority. The state ameliorates the welfare of the unemployed and protects workers on a grand scale. More than ever before, California is the mecca of those who seek recreation, leisure, and comfort. The pendulum of politics swings from right to left. Today Los Angeles is the largest city in the country in area, California the most populous.

More than ever, California seems to be an unpredictable state of mind, a volatile distillation of all that is most American in the United States.

TWO CALIFORNIAS

In California you can move in many worlds that are only a few hours apart. The shore that stretches almost a thousand miles from the Oregon border to the Mexican border changes character frequently and dramatically. Deserts, mountains, forests, valleys offer their diverse climates and memorable scenery. One convenient way to divide the state, often used, is to consider it as Northern and Southern California, defined a bit arbitrarily as to whether the area under consideration is oriented geographically and emotionally toward San Francisco or toward Los Angeles.

San Francisco

Flourishing child of long-gone sea captains and gold seekers, San Francisco is a forty-seven-square-mile peninsula of the State of California, a compact metropolis containing in capsule size most of the best aspects of life in the United States ... and a few vivid reminders of a fairly bawdy beginning. A snub-nosed impudence, San Francisco is flanked on the west by the Pacific, on the north and south by the world's greatest landlocked harbor, San Francisco Bay. Sometimes irreverently referred to as "Baghdad-by-the-Bay," this is a city that multiplies by six the Seven Hills of Rome and emulates that paragon of antiquity in more ways than one. By any standard, San Francisco is a city of paradox: geographically a square city, but in intellectual and cultural attitudes definitely "nonsquare." Native-born or transplanted, San Franciscans demonstrate such feudal loyalty to their town that visitors often gain the impression that San Francisco is quite separate from the State of California.

The fierce and rugged individualism of the San Franciscan has an indelible way of stamping anything and everything that penetrates his city—even the weather. Hypersensitive to critical controversy about fog, the normal San Franciscan will corner you with his honest and earnest assurances that his city's weather is always predictable.

The visitor's salvation is escape to the hills, the cliffs, the promontories, and the beaches. From its heights, San Francisco affords an intoxicating panorama of the surrounding land and sea, with the blinding, forty-mile clarity of a sunny day or with the mystique of an obscuring fog—beguiling with immediate promise. And San Francisco's famous hills—fantastic, incredible, glorious hills—are given the importance they deserve by the writer Herb Caen, San Francisco's devoted chronicler: " 'Take anything from us—our cable cars, our bridges, even our Bay—but leave us our hills!' This might well be the last rallying cry of the embattled San Franciscan, fighting to save his city—his unique, his beloved, his personal city—from the ever-increasing onslaughts of the manic progressives, with their shopping centers, their housing projects, their freeways, and their other plasticized examples of split-level thinking.

"For it is across its many mountains, crags and pinnacles that the city has lived the longest, sung the loudest and faced the winds of the future most courageously. From its hilltops, it has looked down on a burning city and vowed to build even more magnificently. From the old castles on Nob Hill, it has shouted: 'We are rich and strong, and there are no limits to what we can do.' From the tiny wooden houses of Telegraph Hill, the many voices of the artist, the writer, the musician have carried to the ends of the earth. And from the windows of Twin Peaks and Potrero Hill it has gazed, with strange fondness, over the viewtiful city below and murmured, 'This is the only, this is IT.'

"Hills that are cleft in twain, hills that thrust rooftop saloons to uncharted alcoholic heights, hills transversed by tunnels. Hills that have disappeared—like Rincon, which lost its chic and then its head under the Bay Bridge approaches. Hills that are almost forgotten—like Sutro Heights, where a mayor built his castle, strolled through a formal garden of European grandiloquence, and gazed at the ocean. Hills that are practically unknown—like Red Rock, where the young Saroyan sat, the wind ruffling his hair, and scribbled wild short stories in his notebook.

"To some, there is only one hill—'Tee Hill'—Telegraph. To others, any hill is home, as long as it has a view. And to everybody in every section of the city, there is 'Our Hill,' no matter how slight its eminence, no matter whether it has a name or not. In San Francisco, a hill need be no more than a state of mind, affording a slight rise to the spirits, a fresh outlook on the life that parades in the streets below."

San Francisco's topography is uniquely beautiful; nowhere in our known world is there a city so up and down; so round and round, so divertingly different, so fascinating to behold for the first, the last, or the only time—nowhere is there a city so generously rewarding to the eyes of the beholder.

In 1847, by official proclamation, San Francisco became the name of that fabulous port city. It was in the nick of time, at that, for only one year later newspaper editor Sam Brannan came bursting into town with a bottle of gold dust gleaned from a nearby river, the dramatic beginning of the gold stampede that at first all but depopulated the new city. As news of the find trickled outward in all directions, thousands of avid gold seekers thronged into the city of the Golden Gate. Sundry commercial vessels from the ports of Asia and Europe contributed their own opportunists to the swelling tide that restored San Francisco's population to more than 25,000 souls. And to those who for one reason or another remained in the new city, commercial profits put to shame those enjoyed by even the most successful prospectors: laundering at twenty dollars for a few pieces, a lone apple for five dollars, a single egg for one dollar, and a scanty, mealy-bugged loaf of bread for seventy-five cents.

Not all the great fortunes of San Francisco were mined in the fabled gold fields; empires were built on the golden gleanings of the dirty shirts and the hungry bodies that landed exhausted in the emporiums of the landlords and landladies of the day. Great fires set by arsonists, vice and gambling, gangs and Vigilance Committees set the tone of the city. And over the years, San Francisco has emerged shorn of guilt, a stately city of personal independence and industry.

A great era of expansion followed the fires, though it was broken briefly by the excitement of the Civil War. California considered secession from the Union until the idea was vetoed by her legislature. During these years Bret Harte edited the West's first literary magazine, *The Overland Monthly*, Mark Twain lingered here long enough to write one more book, a dozen newspapers were established, and the ornate Victorian palaces of gingerbread were built from the fortunes made in Central Pacific Railroad stock and Comstock silver and gold.

With the completion of the transcontinental railroad in 1869, San Francisco became the railroad as well as the maritime center of the Pacific coast. A traveler from any point between the Mexican and Canadian borders had only to ask for a ticket to "the City," assured that he would be routed to San Francisco. In 1873, San Francisco's clumsy and inadequate horsecars were supplemented by Hallidie's mechanical cable cars, to be joyously utilized by a population that doubled itself in the years between 1870 and 1890.

Despite a severe depression that affected the entire nation in the early 1890s, San Francisco defiantly asserted her self-confidence with the Midwinter Exposition of 1894, a tremendous carnival held in Golden Gate Park. Somehow the city survived the depression, and then the excitement began all over again—with the advent of the Klondike gold rush in 1897. Again, San Franciscans by the hundreds deserted their city for the beckoning lure of gold, just as their forefathers had done. The population suffered depletion for the next three years, but the dawn of 1900 saw San Francisco's future bright with new burgeoning businesses and commercial enterprises, and an expanding population. Now there were more hotels, more restaurants, more laundries, more rooming houses; two-dollar eggs and eight-dollar apples made instant personal fortunes.

From the wreckage of the greatest earthquake in the state's history, which toppled the city on the morning of April 18, 1906, and from the ashes of the fire that burned for three days following, San Francisco came back with a courage that has become legendary.

The city's subsequent westward expansion resulted in an eventual pattern of short blocks east and west, long blocks north and south. In making available some parts of its more centralized urban space, the city stimulated the building of identical houses in long, orderly rows. Reminiscent of old Europe, and altogether charming, some of the houses are built wall to wall, crowding the narrow sidewalks of narrow streets with their raised basement stories and garages.

Since 1849 San Francisco has been the greatest banking center west of Chicago, and with good reason, for it was the trading post for the nation's early gold. But since those early days, the city's prosperity has been solidly founded on its maritime trade. One of the world's finest natural harbors, San Francisco Bay covers an area of 450 square miles, is five to thirteen miles wide with depths up to thirty-six fathoms, and boasts one hundred miles of shoreline and no fewer than six general-cargo ports.

Exciting and exotic, this is home port to cargo ships plying the Orient and the South Seas, to burdened freighters from the east, to luxury liners and tramp steamers, to the great, gray fighting ships of the U.S. Navy, and to a host of busy little tugs, tooting their whistles as they proudly escort the waterborne ambassadors of other nations.

Continuous and restless contact with the nations of the world has made of San Francisco a cosmopolitan city that ranks on an international level with New York, Paris, Lisbon, and London. Successive waves of European immigration, ship jumpers from foreign vessels, Orientals and Polynesians, polyglot leftovers of the Gold Rush era . . . all these have cast San Francisco in the role of mother of many races, many tongues.

Predominant in the minority groups are the Chinese, although more than fifty percent of them are native-born San Franciscans. Pagoda roofs, iron-grilled balconies, and Chinese temples appear side by side with contemporary American structures in San Francisco's Chinatown, the largest Chinese settlement outside the Orient. Here, a Chinese graduate of an American medical school practices in competition with a traditional Chinese herb doctor. Men and women in old-China dress mingle in streets crowded with Westernized Chinese who conform to the latest in Occidental dress. Old men quietly read world news bulletins, laboriously printed by hand in Chinese word symbols. Restaurants cater their ancient Chinese cuisines; shops and bazaars sell tissue-thin porcelains, jade, lacquer work, and delicate jewelry; joss houses and theaters endlessly perform their ancient repertoires; temples invite the pious, and ancestors are honorably served with veneration and worship as in the old days.

On the southern and western slopes of Telegraph Hill is the Latin Quarter, a gourmet's dream of earthly paradise. Italians are most numerous, but French, Spanish, and Mexicans add a piquance to menus, very few of which they print in English. It is to this section of the city that a San Franciscan turns for gustatory delight; deeply imbedded in the local ego is the natural or acquired talent for dining out, a mode of self-expression that the San Franciscan uses to satisfy his sense of being au courant with his world.

"The City" is well known to the great in the entertainment field, a world stage on which hopefuls in the theatrical profession "try" themselves. It is said, "If they like you in 'the City,' they'll like you in the capitals; if they like you in the capitals, they'll love you in the kingdoms; and if they love you in the kingdoms, you can write your own ticket in 'the City.' "

Music and industry, literature and commerce, art and politics—all are contiguous in Baghdad-by-the-Bay. And all are independent of one another in the Babylonian paradox that is modern San Francisco, a city deferential to her great names in countless ways, but especially warm in her welcome to the new challengers of each decade. Culturally elegant, wise and cynical in the ways of the world, naïve and curious as a new-born baby, San Francisco goes her singular and uncrowded path.

For all that her nonexpansible forty-seven square miles are jam-packed with three quarters of a million people, no city in the world can boast a more wonderfully conceived, magnificently created public park. Golden Gate Park sweeps a wide path from the city's heart to the shore of the Pacific. Half a mile wide and four miles long, the park contains man-made lakes and canyons, brooks and waterfalls, bandstands and stadiums, baseball diamonds and tennis courts, a buffalo reservation, a planetarium and an aquarium—more than a thousand acres of high-priced real estate devoted to the pastoral pleasures of San Franciscans.

San Francisco is old, but is ever young in vitality, like Cleopatra, of whom Shakespeare's Enobarbus said, "Age cannot wither her, nor custom stale her infinite variety." Roaming cautiously up and down and around her contoured hills, you may prefer to trust life and limb to a hired and experienced driver—or to your own two feet. Or, rejecting caution, you may drive your car through charming cul de sacs and labyrinthian turnings. Being sensible, you can see all of fascinating San Francisco from the air-conditioned safety of tourist buses. This wonderful city varies in altitude from sea level to 933.6 feet above sea level, and every inch can be explored with unforgettable delight.

Nob Hill, once the retreat of the gold-rich "nabobs," has given way to Pacific Heights, the *ne plus ultra* of social eminence; to Telegraph Hill, intellectual stronghold of the San Franciscans, and to the exclusive neighborhoods of Sea Cliff, the Marina, and Russian Hill. A visit to this modern Babylon is pure frustration without at least one sampling of Filbert Street, swooping down its 37.1-percent grade from Hyde at the top to Leavenworth at the bottom. San Franciscans are well satisfied with this street's name, claiming that only a nut would drive its spectacular descent. Then there's the less frightening but equally breakneck course of Lombard Street, famed afar as the crookedest street in the world. All the way down from Hyde, Lombard corkscrews in a wild series of nearly ninety-degree turns — gorgeously landscaped but definitely not recommended for the faint-hearted driver.

The mere name San Francisco evokes the image of these steeply sloping streets, complete with the ubiquitous cable cars of which three lines (and several dozen cars) remain in daily operation. A 15-cent ride on any one of their routes makes a native of the most casual visitor, affording him a bone-jarring and traditional introduction to the city's most charming and best-known points of interest. Fisherman's Wharf, Nob Hill, Russian Hill, Aquatic Park, Chinatown, Grace Cathedral, its gilt bronze doors cast from the Ghiberti doors of the baptistry in Florence, the Mark Hopkins and Fairmont Hotels, and the old Federal prison, Alcatraz—all can be seen during one cable-car trip, "briefing" the visitor for a more leisurely return, which is inevitable for those caught up in San Francisco's fascination.

Opulent, proud of her grande dame decadence, San Francisco is unabashed by a seamier side which presents the usual big-city acquisitions of slums and poverty pockets. Indeed, her luxury hotels are more than ever a vital part of the city's essential character and, since the Gold Rush, have never ceased to be a source of wonder and pleasure to visitors and residents. From the days of Ralston's Palace Hotel—a vulgar extravaganza built in 1875, destroyed by the 1906 fire, and rebuilt shortly after—to her present eminence, San Francisco has enjoyed the reputation of having on a per capita basis the nation's largest selection of first-class hotel accommodations, as well as superlative convention facilities.

Noting the exaggerated pre-opening claims of the Palace's management, one 1875 columnist, definitely in the Mark Twain tradition, bemused his readers by estimating "the ground covered by the Palace Hotel to be eleven hundred and fifty-four square miles, six yards, two inches and ha'penny farthing, or say a space equal to the states of Wisconsin and Rhode Island, and the right-hand half of Senegambia.... The ponderous weight of the entire edifice, that is, when full, accounts for the recent singular bulge noticed in the earth near Shanghai, China, within a few months past.... A contract is already given out for the construction of a flume from the Yosemite to conduct the Bridal Veil fall thither, and which it is designed to have pour over the east front.... The beds are made with Swiss watch springs and stuffed with camel's hair, each single hair costing eleven cents by the wholesale.... There are thirty-four elevators in all — four for passengers, ten for baggage and twenty for mixed drinks. Each elevator contains a piano and a bowling alley.... All the entrees will be sprinkled with gold dust, and every ninth pie will contain a pearl as large as a wren's egg...."

Although modern San Francisco hostelries make no such immodest claims, the best ones still operate on the theory that gold in any form, and by any name, is acceptable today.

Aside from tourism on a grandiose scale, her function as a water way-station for the United States Navy, and her role of international gateway to and from the Orient, the major export of San Francisco is—San Francisco!

An unbelievable city with an incredible past, San Francisco is complex and all-American, a city of romantic imagination, a city that never suffered the pangs of urban adolescence, a sophisticated and generous mother to the nation's creative refugees, and a stronghold for the naïve and the disenchanted.

Now removed from early Spanish influence, the city is yet predominantly Catholic in religion; French, Italian, Mexican, and Chinese in gastronomy; eclectic and emotional in her ethnic attitudes, and altogether insular in her rejection of outside interference. And consistent with her paradoxical nature, San Francisco's snobbish condescension to the outlander is canceled out by her warmly open welcome to the instant tourist who stays to become yet another worldly and vivacious San Franciscan. And a word of caution: no faster way has ever been invented to empty a room of San Franciscans than to say, "Los Angeles' climate is a little better than Frisco's." Right there, in one innocent statement, you will have lost every potential friend in Baghdad-by-the-Bay, for "Los Angeles" is anathema to San Franciscans, and "Frisco" is an unadulterated insult of abbreviations!

The Bay area Cities

Across the bay from San Francisco are the cities of Oakland and Berkeley. Oakland is a vigorous industrial center and port and the fourth-largest city in California. Berkeley is a cultural center compassing the University of California and campus. Both are known for their beautiful homes, which adorn the low hills of the area. The view from Skyline Boulevard, which rides the crest of the Berkeley Hills, offers an impressive vista of the entire Golden Gate country. Slightly warmer than San Francisco and less foggy, Oakland-Berkeley tends toward informality in dress and atmosphere. Light, pastel-tinted dresses and sports shirts blossom as soon as the weather permits.

The Bay area cities are linked to San Francisco by the San Francisco-Oakland Bay Bridge. Freeways and tunnels connect Oakland in every other direction. These cities are home to commuters who work in San Francisco, to industries and their workers, and to one of the world's great universities, and all that that implies, these days. Behind Oakland and Berkeley and their neighbors—San Leandro, Hayward, Emeryville, Piedmont, and Alameda—rise the low Berkeley Hills to almost 2,000 feet. These wooded slopes parallel the shore, and homes are built on them as in Naples. There the resemblance ends. Count the trees of camphor, acacia, pepper, eucalyptus, and palm. A drive down the Skyline Boulevard, which winds along the wooded Berkeley Hills, with the dry higher range on the Contra Costa Hills rising some thirty miles to the east, caresses the eye.

Oakland is a fine, busy town, which has learned the art of combining homes and industry. In 1955 the Kaiser Center arose, the fifty-million-dollar home of the Kaiser Industrial empire. A coliseum and cultural center designed by Eero Saarinen and Associates are being added. Beautiful Lakeside Park stands above Lake Merritt, once a mud flat. The Oakland Naval Supply Center provides material needs for all ships of the U.S. Navy in the Pacific and Far East area. The U.S. Navy looms big around here, with the Naval Air station just across the waterway in Alameda.

Berkeley

Berkeley, bordering on the east shore of San Francisco facing the Golden Gate, is named for that Irish Bishop Berkeley who said, "Westward, the course of empire takes its way!" A trustee of the College of California back in the nineteenth century thought the idea was so good that the name was adopted by the trustees of the college town where the buildings of the University of California stand.

Here campus rebels are possibly stimulated by contrasts. Old houses with steep-pitched roofs, single-sided, climb the hills. Sprinkled among the early rustic architecture are modern stucco houses and apartments. The houses are strung along the hill, with a wonderful bay view, and some look over into canyons behind. Along the waterfront, Berkeley is a business and industrial center. Many commuters go to work in San Francisco. Berkeley has a tradition of splendid civic pride.

The spacious University of California campus is a beautifully landscaped park. First there was an academy there in 1853, then a college in 1860. In 1869, the college became a university and in 1870 coeducational. From these beginnings, California's splendid system of colleges and universities has grown.

Sacramento

Quite properly, Sacramento, northeast of San Francisco in the heart of the Central Valley, became the state's capital in 1854. It was here, on a fifty-thousand-acre grant which a Swiss ex-army officer had taken up earlier by swearing allegiance to the Mexican flag, that gold was found in 1848. Sutter's Fort, the stronghold of Johann Augustus Sutter, was the mecca of the western world for a few years thereafter. The gold found on his property ruined him. Gold seekers overran him, staked claims on his land, and stole his cattle. He moved to Pennsylvania in 1873.

The Pony Express came through Sacramento, and this city was a terminus of the first railroad in California. Sacramento storekeepers of the 1870s controlled the state for forty years thereafter — Leland Stanford, Collis P. Huntington, Mark Hopkins, and Charles Crocker.

Sacramento County and the fertile Sacramento Valley are important agriculturally. Two rivers, the American and the Sacramento, meet here. A deep-water channel to Suisun on San Francisco Bay was completed in the 1960s. Principal industries are the Aerojet-General Corporation and the Douglas Aircraft Company. McClellan Air Force Base and Mather Air Force Base are nearby. Sailing, water skiing and boating on Lake Folsom and Nimbus Lake, and fishing and hunting in the great forests to the east in the Sierras are popular recreations.

North of San Francisco, across the Golden Gate Bridge, is Marin County and the suburban towns of Sausalito, Belvedere, Mill Valley, San Anselmo, and Novato. Scenic woods, attractive beaches, and fishing and boating facilities constitute the main charms of this area. As the panorama of San Francisco's skyline fades behind, old lighthouses, dramatic offshore rocks, and picturesque little art colonies appear, in contrast to luxurious residential towns such as Belvedere.

Mount Tamalpais overlooks the Bay in sylvan elegance. Muir Woods National Monument, adjacent to Mount Tamalpais State Park, preserves a cool stand of virgin redwoods at the foot

Santa Catalina Island

This plate combines the bucolic and maritime features of a lovely town, aptly called Avalon, where most of the island's population resides. Santa Catalina (Saint Catherine) Island lies twenty-nine miles from Los Angeles and is 22 miles long and 8 miles wide. It is reached by motor cruiser (two and a half hours) and often by airplane.

Discovered by Juan Rodríguez Cabrillo in 1542, in the early days the island was a rendezvous for pirates and smugglers. Fine beaches, jutting pier, challenging golf course and, of course, the thrills of deep-sea fishing are exciting features of life on this island today. Although it is now being commercially developed, the island retains all the attractiveness that makes it a magnet for visitors and for residents of Los Angeles.

SOUTHERN CALIFORNIA

San Diego de Alcalá, where California started

On a hill overlooking Mission Valley the white buildings greet the visitor long before he reaches the mission on his six-mile drive from San Diego. The most pictorial part of this first mission — the Mother Mission of California (1769) — is the *campanario* or belltower. The picture shows a view from the gardens. The original tower collapsed a century ago, but it has been beautifully reconstructed with five bells, of which the largest, the Mater Dolorosa, was cast in 1894 from an original set of five bells which were given to the mission by the Viceroy.

Mission San Luis Rey de Francia

Situated on a hill overlooking Highway 76, which leads east from Oceanside, this stately old mission, founded in 1798, was once the largest and richest of all California missions. The picture shows the front entrance of the church facing east and the highway. Planned and built from 1811 to 1815, this elaborate cruciform church has a dome over the crossing. This is the only dome remaining among the California missions. Old trees frame the view, with the old fountain in the middle ground.

Father Serra's Church, San Juan Capistrano

Built in 1777, this is the oldest church in California still in use. In fact, it is California's oldest building, and is the only church in existence in which Father Serra celebrated Mass. The baroque altar that so effectively decorates this old adobe chapel is possibly a bit older than the church. It was brought from Spain and installed in 1923. Of great interest are the Indian designs on the ceiling and walls, visible in the picture.

Mission San Luis Rey de Francia: Laundry and Orchards

There is a wide stairway leading between the orchards to the laundry where the Indians washed and cleaned the garments of the mission inhabitants. A supply of water was provided by an intricate water system (see spout-head in the picture), which is one of the many historic attractions of the mission.

The Pacific Coast of Southern California

Multicolored ice plants and other blooms of breathtaking beauty frame the white sands and the blue, green, and white foam from the gentle sea. This is an unspoiled haven for anyone seeking that rare combination of the spiritual and material joys provided by nature on land and in the sea.

View from Mount Wilson

Except for aerial views, seldom are such vistas of a city possible. But because Los Angeles is overlooked by majestic mountains, one can look from high points such as Mount Wilson upon a goodly portion of this sprawling community, its outlying districts, and the Pacific Ocean in the background.

Beach at La Jolla

La Jolla is mainly a residential district within the corporate limits of San Diego. Besides its beautiful homes, it has a famous and picturesque coastline full of coves, small sandy beaches, caves, and cliffs. On the cliffs, some very attractive houses have been built.

In Palm Springs

Palm Springs is in the Colorado Desert, at the foot of San Jacinto Peak. Its mineral springs have been popular for many years, and its warm winters and dry desert areas have caused it to be the winter residence of thousands of people, including General Dwight D. Eisenhower and Bob Hope. With its canyons, museums, and nationally known golf tournaments, Palm Springs is a lure for travelers from all over the world, but also very popular with Angelenos, who can reach it in a two-hour drive.

Skyline from Point Loma, San Diego

Point Loma is a modern residential area, looking over the bay to downtown San Diego. The first white man to land here was Juan Rodriguez Cabrillo, in 1542, and today San Diego is a big city, a manufacturing and shipping center with a metropolitan-area population of about 1,000,000.

*Residential section,
Palm Springs*

Palm Springs has a beautiful residential section, ranch-type and modern homes with desert gardens. The picture shows snowcapped San Jacinto Peak (10,831 ft.) in the background.

Pauma Indian Cemetery, Pala

Situated within the limits of an old sub-mission, San Antonio de Pala, the Indian cemetery looks quite romantic, with its belltower in the center. It is the only originally detached belltower among the missions. Two stories in height, it was built away from the church because by this time California earthquakes were notorious for sending bells crashing through church roofs. This *campanario* did, in fact, fall in 1916 but has since been rebuilt.

Summer at Lake Arrowhead

This idyllic scene shows a portion of Lake Arrowhead. The lake, situated at an altitude of more than 5,000 feet, is two and a half miles long and a mile wide and is part of the San Bernardino National Forest.

On Mount Wilson:
View Toward San Gabriel
Mountains

This picture shows the beautiful mountains and forests in the immediate neighborhood of Los Angeles. The famous astronomical observatory is situated here and houses some of the finest telescopes for cosmic observation in the world.

Church Ruins: San Juan Capistrano

An hour's drive south from Los Angeles will take you to the town of San Juan Capistrano. The old mission is in the center of town. The picture shows the impressive ruins of the great stone church, completed in 1806. It was once the largest of all California mission churches, 146 feet long and 28 feet wide. It took nine years to build, and the work was done mostly by the Indians, who brought its heavy stones from a quarry six miles away. The impressive building, with its 120-foot-high belltower crowning the front entrance, collapsed in an earthquake (1812). Forty people died in the tragic accident. The bells, however, were saved and mounted into a wall of the mission gardens.

Newport Beach Yacht Basin

At Newport Beach is one of the great yachting marinas of the Pacific Coast, more than 7,500 registered boats and yachts being berthed here. The city itself comprises Balboa, Balboa Island, Lido Isle, Corona del Mar, Newport Heights, Harbor Island, Bay Shores, and Linda Isle and includes a six-mile sandy beach. It can be reached in less than an hour from the center of Los Angeles.

Wayfarer Chapel, Palos Verdes

Designed by Lloyd Wright, son of the illustrious architect Frank Lloyd Wright, the Wayfarer Chapel seems part of the out-of-doors. It is almost entirely of glass and is set in an enchanting sea-cliff setting, a haven for prayer and meditation.

Disneyland, Anaheim

Disneyland is a dream come true. Depictions of the Old West, rides on stagecoach through the Painted Desert, startling ventures into the future, and many other adventures afford a genuine treat for every member of the family.

Laguna Beach

Laguna Beach, like Carmel-by-the-Sea, is a haven for artists and landscape painters. It has superb scenery, quaint rustic dwellings, lovely beaches and coves and rolling hills covered with colorful gardens. Laguna Beach combines many of the lovely coastal features typical of Southern California.

Buena Park:
Panning Gold at Knott's Berry Farm

To visit this farm, where admission is free, is
to be transported backward in history to "the
good old days of the ghost town." It began as
a little roadside berry stand, and today it is
a historical and educational landmark providing endless enjoyment for many thousands of
people. There are 60 acres for free parking,
restaurants, and ghost town with its gold mine,
wagon camp, railroad, cable cars, and 1500
courteous employees devoted to the visitor's
pleasure. One can pan gold dust to take home,
just as in 1849. Knott's Berry Farm is near
Disneyland.

Long Beach

The city, fifth largest in California (population 345,000),
is an important industrial center and a home port of the
U.S. Navy. With its beautiful eight-mile beach, five golf
courses, pier, and deepsea fishing, it is a sports center
of Southern California. This
view, taken from a semicircu-
lar pier, shows the weekday
serenity of the beach, which
throbs with activity on week-
ends.

In Pasadena

In the seclusion of the foot-hills of the San Gabriel Mountains lies Pasadena. It is connected with the center of Los Angeles by the Pasadena Freeway. Noted as a winter resort and famed for its parks, golf courses, and tennis courts, Pasadena has for one of its chief claims to fame the renowned Rose Bowl, where the annual New Year's Day football game is played, following the spectacular Tournament of Roses. But Pasadena also has a playhouse, a famous art museum, and the renowned California Institute of Technology. Nearby is the Mount Wilson Observatory.

Pasadena City Hall

Few areas in America can boast of a city hall that is so truly a Spanish monument. Presiding over a populace of more than 100,000, this civic edifice at the foot of the San Gabriel Mountains is a venerable and charming landmark of the past and an active civic center of the present.

View from Palos Verdes

Palos Verdes, an elegant residential community, is situated in the south-western outskirts of Los Angeles. High up on a hill between San Pedro and Redondo Beach, it offers a beautiful view along the coast. To the north are the beaches: Redondo, Hermosa, Manhattan.

The Famous Freeways of Los Angeles

This maze of concrete ribbons, threading its devious ways in and out of Los Angeles, has set a pattern for many modern metropolitan areas. On the lower level, shown here, is one of the finest examples, the Harbor Freeway. The best-known freeways are Harbor, San Diego, Hollywood, Pasadena, Ventura, Golden State, Santa Monica, Santa Ana, and San Bernardino freeways. Plans call for continuous construction of new freeways, some of which are almost completed.

Los Angeles City Hall

Although Los Angeles is a city of many showplaces, Angelenos are proud of their modern, 32-story City Hall. Built in 1926, it occupies an entire city block, and from its tower it affords an excellent view of the Los Angeles area and points beyond.

University of California at Los Angeles

Established in 1919, the university started in an area devoted to beans and grains. Now, with a student enrollment in excess of 23,000, it ranks with the great universities of the world. Its architecture runs a colorful gamut from Italian Renaissance, in some of the original buildings, to such starkly modern and more functional buildings of recent construction as the one shown in this photograph.

Griffith Park, with Observatory and Roosevelt Golf Course

This panoramic view shows the Roosevelt Golf Course in the foreground and the city of Los Angeles in the distance. Between, high on a cliff at the right, is the famous Griffith Observatory and Planetarium. Here, by means of a giant projector, the stars and galaxies are made visible to the naked eye. Also reproduced are such startling effects as the hues of sunrises and sunsets, eclipses, the Northern Lights, and planets. Griffith Park—a tract of 4,253 acres—is the largest municipal park in the United States.

Theme Building at Los Angeles International Airport

At this airport one finds, in a setting more modern than tomorrow, a unique structure called "The Theme." It is a revolving restaurant, designed for dazzling scenic delights and gastronomic thrills.

Hollywood and Los Angeles

Los Angeles, of which Hollywood is a part, is today the largest city in the United States. It was founded in 1781 by Don Felipe de Neve, Spanish governor of California, as the Pueblo de Nuestra Señora la Reina de los Angeles. The center of this very modern city is still Spanish, especially around famous Olvera Street, the old plaza church, and the town square. The city grew immensely after two railroad lines reached Los Angeles from the East (1876 and 1885). It is still growing at a phenomenal rate. The interesting picture was taken from the hills behind Hollywood and shows the expanse to the west and the Pacific coast.

Mission San Gabriel Arcángel

Strange, perhaps, that a mission so stark and fortresslike should stand in the midst of modern-day hubbub and activity. Yet, with its ancient tower bells and picturesque fountains, lawn, and hedges, it remains apart from its urban surroundings.

Hollywood and Hollywood Bowl

With the night lights of Hollywood glittering in the background, we see a bird's-eye view of the famous Hollywood Bowl. The natural amphitheater is the locale for many concerts and ballets. The concert season begins in the second week of July, and at Easter thousands of worshipers attend the colorful and inspiring Sunrise Service.

*Historic Avila Adobe,
Los Angeles*

In Los Angeles there are many places, outside museums, where one can feast one's eyes on the charms of bygone eras. One such sight is Avila Adobe on Olvera Street. Built about 1818 by Don Francisco Avila, it became the headquarters of many notable characters in American history, including General Frémont and the illustrious Kit Carson.

*New Music Center
for the Performing Arts,
Los Angeles*

Los Angeles has been a leading sponsor in the promotion of music. The Woman's Symphony Orchestra of Los Angeles was organized in 1895, and in 1919 the Los Angeles Philharmonic Orchestra. Through the ensuing years, new musical attractions have been added. This complex is at the crown of the Civic Center. The view shown here captures some of the excitement of what takes place within—opera, symphony, chamber music, musical comedies, and ballet.

A Street named Olvera, Los Angeles

This was the city's birthplace, and it still reflects the spirit of Old Mexico. The quaint booths, shops, and cafés—indoor and sidewalk types—simulate a realistic Mexican market.

Los Angeles County Museum of Art

The attractive modern exterior of this magnificent museum gives exciting promise of the rare delights contained inside. Three buildings, connected by covered walks, open onto a large exhibition area for sculpture. The galleries house a splendid permanent collection from prehistoric art through the arts of Western civilization and the Orient.

San Fernando Valley

In living color, this photograph shows the great valley, compassing 258 square miles and a considerable area of residential and business communities. In June there is the spectacular San Fernando Valley Fiesta.

Los Angeles City Public Library

Virtually across the street from the Biltmore Hotel, where John F. Kennedy won the Democratic nomination for the Presidency in 1960, this is one of the best libraries in the world. Founded in 1872, it contains more than 1,100,000 volumes and brings its services to all the neighboring libraries and to all the residents of Los Angeles County through its modern Bookmobiles.

Huntington Library, San Marino

This beautiful building is part of the Huntington Library and Art Gallery in San Marino, a suburb of Los Angeles. Its founder was Henry E. Huntington. Situated in a 207-acre park, which surrounds the buildings of the Library and Art Gallery, the Huntington Library is considered one of the finest in the world, with a famous collection of manuscripts, letters, and documents including the Gutenberg Bible of 1455, Benjamin Franklin's Autobiography, Mark Twain's "The Prince and the Pauper". Not all are on permanent display. Among the letters are some by George Washington and a printed version of Columbus's letter announcing the discovery of America.

Chinatown—Downtown

This is a colorful corner of Chinatown, one of the most interesting sections of the city of Los Angeles. No visitor should pass up the opportunity that is presented to "go East." The new Chinatown is successor to the original Chinatown, destroyed by an earthquake.

Great Western Divide

The picture is taken looking out from Moro Rock in the Sequoia National Park. California encloses the highest, after Alaska, and the lowest points in the United States: Mount Whitney (14,495 feet), within the limits of Sequoia National Park, and, just behind the Great Western Divide in Death Valley, the lowest point, 282 feet below sea level. The picture shows one of the many beautiful views in the Sequoia National Park extending to the Western Divide.

Giant Sequoia

This is one of the famous trees in Sequoia National Park. Just compare the human figure in the lower right part of the picture with the size of the tree. *Sequoia (gigantea)* are among the oldest living things in the world. By ring count, some are about 3500 years old, and they have a diameter of 20 to 30 feet and a height of 250 feet and more. They are found not only in this National Park but in about 35 other groves in California.

Sunset on Mt. Whitney, Highest Mountain in California (14,495 feet)

Looking west from the picturesque Ala-bama Hills near Lone Pine, one sees the High Sierra with Mount Whitney in the center, the highest mountain in the United States outside Alaska.

San Antonio Peak: View of the Mojave Desert

The southeastern part of California is desert—the Mojave Desert—a lonesome region of fantastic formations. It was at one time covered with ocean, then lifted to considerable heights (2000 to 5000 feet) and covered with lava and ashes. The mountains are colored in chocolate brown, gray, and lavender. Seen from a distance, they have a bluish tinge. A vast land of silence, intense heat, and unusual sporadic vegetation, the desert blooms in February and March in brillant colors.

In contrast, the green mountain ranges to the southwest of the desert offer beautiful views —like the one pictured here from Mt. San Antonio over the Mojave Desert. Note that the trees disappear in the background, enhancing the spaciousness of these colored wastelands.

San Fernando Rey de España, San Fernando

The picture shows how much alive this mission is once again today. Photographed on a Sunday during mass, the old church is filled to capacity. This picture also shows—particularly at the right—the irregular sloping of the walls due to the primitive workmanship.

The gardens and the adjoining city park are beautiful; they separate the mission from the busy traffic of suburban Los Angeles. As a matter of fact, the suburb bears the name of the mission—San Fernando.

Lompoc: Mission La Purísima Concepción

This mission is a state historical monument and is the most complete historic restoration in the West, providing us with a clear picture of how the Indians worked in this settlement, and how they practiced such crafts as processing hides, baking bread, and candlemaking. The picture above shows one of the old olive trees behind the mission fountain.

Santa Barbara, Queen of the California Missions

Considered the best-preserved and architecturally most attractive of all California missions, it has influenced the whole appearance of the city of Santa Barbara. Even the most modern buildings are cast in the Spanish style, making this community one of the most beautiful in California. This Queen of the missions was built in 1815 to replace an older building founded in 1786. The style is Spanish-Moorish. The stately structure of the church and the well-designed buildings around it are truly imposing. The surrounding scenery is equally beautiful. The whole is situated on a hill commanding a lovely view of Santa Barbara. Father Serra himself was of the opinion that this location was an earthly paradise. This mission has been in continuous use since its dedication by Father Lasuén in 1786. It closely resembles its original appearance, although it, too, experienced earthquakes, Indian wars, fires, bandit raids, and Mexican battles.

*Old Olive Press,
Mission San Miguel
Arcángel*

This eye-catching mission, with its attractive buildings, walls, and ruins, and a quite newly constructed belltower close to Highway 101, was once a thriving Indian agricultural community under mission guidance. Many of the old instruments and machinery are still on exhibition here, such as the olive press, which the picture shows. Picturesque indeed are the surrounding walls (also partly visible in the background of the picture), with interesting little towers and niches.

*San Luis Obispo: The Old
Mission Church (1772)*

The fifth mission founded by Father Serra stands in the center of the city of the same name, which developed around it. As the picture clearly shows, the mission is in an elevated situation. The church bears the year of its founding (1772). It is well preserved and serves as a parish church for the many Catholics of the city. Behind the church is a romantic garden.

San Simeon: Neptune Pool

One of the great showplaces of California is the San Simeon State Historical Monument, formerly the home of the late William Randolph Hearst. It is a glamorous composite of mansions, sculptures, and pools situated in beautiful gardens. It is situated off the coastal road between Monterey and Morro Bay, on top of La Cuesta Encantada —The Enchanted Hill—on the western slopes of the Coast Range. La Casa Grande, looking like an imposing church, overlooks the buildings and terraced gardens. One of the most beautiful spots at the western approach is the Neptune Pool, with its Greek temple, as shown in the picture. The Hearst San Simeon Historical Monument is within the Piedra Blanca Rancho (40,000 acres) bought by Senator George Hearst in 1865. William Randolph Hearst, creator of the fabulous newspaper empire, developed the part that is now the State Historical Monument and which was deeded to the State of California.

Mission San Antonio de Padua, Jolon

Located within the Hunter Liggett Military Reservation, home of the California National Guard, the mission can easily be reached from Highway 101 (about twenty miles from King City) or with difficulty from California State Highway 1, five miles south of Santa Lucía. It is one of the most completely restored missions again in working condition. It is also a training school for Franciscan brothers, who learn here the skills of mission industries as well as modern trades. The upper picture shows the belltower and entrance to the church, an unusual combination but quite attractive, with its double façade and the adjoining arches to the left.

This mission has most of the old industries and workshops in well-preserved condition, such as the blacksmith shop pictured in the lower photograph.

Salt Figures on Mono Lake

It's a strange lake and the third-largest in California. Also it looks beautiful, blue, and inviting. There is no life in Mono Lake except some small salt-water shrimp; there are no fish, no plants. The reason is that the water is saturated with alkaline substances, which pile up on the shores of the 87 square miles of water like a soapy foam and, in places, especially on the northwestern shore, they have built these peculiar figures, ten to twenty feet high. Mono Lake, at a surface elevation of 6409 feet, is near Tioga Pass, eastern entrance of Yosemite National Park, and 25 miles south of Bridgeport.

Shooting Stars in Bloom

In early July the meadows of the Sierra Nevada are ablaze with the pink of the Shooting Stars (*Dodecatheon vadicatum*). These spectacular heralds of summer glow pink when viewed in profusion but actually have a sharp black beak, touches of white, and spots of butter yellow.

Mammoth Lakes

The popular resort area of Mammoth Lakes includes more than 30 lakes in a basin about 9,000 feet high. It's a fisherman's paradise, in beautiful mountain surrounding. Lake Mary, Twin Lakes, Lake George, and Horseshoe Lake are the best known; they can be reached on good roads from the main highway between Bishop and Lee Vining.

Sunset on the Pacific Coast
(Santa Monica)

A typical view of the Pacific Ocean off Southern California, with the silhouette of a palm and some cactus.

of the mountain. These are the coast redwoods *(Sequoia sempervirens),* kept always green by the rolling fog. The largest tree here is 246 feet high and seventeen feet in width.

In Stinson Beach State Park, swimmers brave the chilly surf, fishermen make good catches, and clam diggers bring home the supper. About thirty miles north of San Francisco is Point Reyes National Seashore, idyllic and picturesque, with forest headland, bay, and beach that offer picturesque weekend retreats for those who want to get away from it all.

Point Reyes National Seashore was created in 1962, and since that date a slow process of land acquisition has been taking place. In the original act, some 64,000 acres were to be acquired here. The highway out to Drake's Bay is a splendid one, and traffic is usually light. There are picturesque beaches (mostly for sunning and walking; the surf is treacherous for swimming).

In 1579 Sir Francis Drake, on his way around the world and to fame and fortune and a meeting with the Spanish Armada, is supposed to have paused here to careen his ship, the *Golden Hind.* The Indians, awed by the white men, venerated Drake.

The coarse-sand beaches are littered with driftwood and alive with sea birds. The old Coast Guard lighthouse is being abandoned after long years of service. There is an adjacent state park, miles of hiking trails, wooded regions to explore.

Saluted in prose and poetry, the Point Reyes country is some of the finest in Northern California.

Farther north the coastal highway crosses Russian River, with rural roads leading up into apple and dairy-farming country, orchards and vineyards, and hop fields to the east. This river resort bustles by summer, and fishermen love it in the winter when the steelhead run.

State Highway 1 winds north over highlands to Fort Ross, a state historical monument, a reconstruction of the Russian outpost built here early in the nineteenth century. Here in 1812 Russian traders and Aleut hunters established a settlement guarded by two-story blockhouses, and hoped to find food for the starving settlement of Russians at Sitka, Alaska. In the end the settlement was a failure, partly because of the extermination of the sea otter along the coast. In 1824 Russia agreed to limit future settlement to Alaska.

Farther north is the Mendocino Coast, a wild and rocky run of Pacific coastline. Here is the artist colony community of Mendocino, the fishing community of Noyo, the lumbering town of Fort Bragg. Then the fine beach-following highway curves back to U.S. Highway 101 inland. Left almost to the locals is the rugged, dirt-road country called the Mattole—some of Northern California's least-known coastal area.

Redwood Country

Several state parks, a newly acquired area of the National Park system, and some private land make up the new Redwoods National Park, born in 1968. It will highlight a sprawling region where the sequoia grows tall and beautiful. Many of the redwood groves have been cut by logging interests. Conservationists fought long and hard to save some of the virgin redwood forests for posterity. Many of the redwood groves can be seen from Highway 101. To enjoy fully the silence and the splendor of the groves, one has to park one's car, lose oneself in the ruddy forest, and listen to the wind in the ancient 200- and 300-foot-tall trees.

The Wine Country

Northern California's wine country is situated largely in Sonoma and Napa counties, seventy-five miles north of San Francisco. Here Buena Vista Vineyards was founded in 1856 by Colonel Agoston Haraszthy, a Hungarian nobleman, who set out grape cuttings from all over Europe. September is the time to watch the harvest, enjoy a tour of the wineries, and go to Sonoma Valley's Moon Vintage Festival in the last weekend of the month to celebrate the grape harvest.

Santa Rosa

Northeast of San Francisco on U.S. Highway 101 is Santa Rosa, where Luther Burbank planted and experimented for half a century. His home and gardens are here, and the Luther Burbank Rose Festival is held here each year in May. Nearby is a noble state historical monument, Vallejo's Petaluma Adobe, a 66,000-acre rancho and hacienda dating back to the days of the Spaniards. It is the largest and grandest adobe structure in Northern California, open to visitors, with a ranger on duty to show them around.

Clear Lake

Clear Lake, the largest body of water entirely within California, lies about 110 miles north, and a little west, of Oakland. Nineteen miles long, fairly shallow, it is a favorite summer resort.

Eureka

The largest town in California north of Sacramento is Eureka, on Humboldt Bay. After being stationed here in 1854, Captain Ulysses S. Grant resigned from the U.S. Army because he was depressed by it. Eureka is the setting for Peter B. Kyne's story "Valley of the Giants." On nearby Indian Island, in 1860, white settlers massacred all the Indian women and children and elders in 1860, and when Bret Harte wrote in horror of what they had done, he had to leave town. The Eureka people also ran the Chinese out of town in 1885 and took their land. Despite this dark past, Eureka is a fine town on a beautiful shore today, with great redwoods nearby and splendid fishing. Lumber, plywood manufacturing, and fish processing and curing are the chief industries.

San Jose

The metropolis of Santa Clara Valley is San Jose, about seven miles south of San Francisco Bay and one of the thriving residential towns of the Bay area. It was the first Spanish settlement, as distinguished from the missions, in Alta California. The sleepy pueblo town became a supply city in the gold rush and was briefly the capital of the state in 1849. The capital was moved to Benicia in 1851 and thence to Sacramento in 1854.

Today San Jose is both an industrial city and the center of big vegetable, fruit, and walnut productions. One third of the world's prunes come from this county. A fascinating tourist attraction is the Winchester Mystery House, built over a period of thirty-eight years by the widow of a son of the man who invented the Winchester rifle. She had become a spiritualist, and she believed that as long as she kept on building her home she would never die. The 160-room mansion that rambles over six acres is the result. There are miles of crooked halls leading nowhere, trapdoors, doors opening to the sky, a grand ballroom that never had a ball.

The Monterey Peninsula and Carmel

A hundred miles south of San Francisco are two of the most entrancing communities in California. These are historic Monterey and Carmel-by-the-Sea. The seventeen-mile drive winding along the coast around Monterey peninsula is memorable.

Monterey, state capital from 1775 to 1846, has picturesque Spanish colonial structures on nearly every street. It is still a fishing town, whose pungently aromatic streets have been immortalized in John Steinbeck's novels. Cannery Row, celebrated by Steinbeck, is today much frequented by artists, writers, and tourists. For thirty years it was the center of the canning of the true silver sardine. Here, 234,163 tons of sardines were put into cans in 1945, and in the same year the fish disappeared from nearby waters. The fleet moved south. Galleries, restaurants, shops, and theaters have replaced the canneries.

The drive curves through the exclusive Pebble Beach playground, golf capital of the world, where the fairways extend to the sea's edge and where Bing Crosby sponsors the far-famed National Pro-Amateur Championship.

South of Carmel is Point Lobos State Park, a wild and rocky point where sea lions throng. They gave the place its Spanish name, Punta de Los Marinos (point of the sea wolves). Sea lions sun themselves and bark on the offshore rocks all about Monterey Bay.

Pacific Grove, a thriving community and resort at the southern tip of Monterey Bay, is host each winter to thousands of Monarch butterflies that fly south in the fall. It is against the law to injure a butterfly here, and the penalty for doing so is a $500 fine. Ducks, geese, and gulls abound around Monterey peninsula and flock when fed with crumbs. Monterey cypresses cling to the rocky shoreline. The peninsula also boasts the only processing plant on the Pacific Coast that washes and dries sand for bathing beaches.

Carmel faces the open Pacific in a forest at the southern tip of the Monterey Peninsula. Father Junípero Serra is buried at Mission Carmel, beautifully and accurately restored. Starting out as a retreat for artists, Carmel still retains its bohemian atmosphere in spite of heavy tourist infiltration. In pursuit of the peaceful, cultural life, Carmel avoids house numbers, mail delivery, the glare of neon, and unnecessary street lights. The city has many smart shops, which offer luxury specialties of every kind. Carmel's great crescent-shaped beach enhances the picturesqueness of this residential community.

Big Sur

About twenty-five miles south of Carmel, the highway enters the Big Sur country, beloved of poets and writers and anyone else who is enchanted with a wild and rocky shore, tempestuous winds, and handsome redwoods. The drive along the coast is breath-taking and Point Sur Lighthouse dramatic. Henry Miller has a home here. Robinson Jeffers has written poems and Jack Kerouac novels about the Big Sur country, but probably the lines that best describe it are: "Ye ways where surges roar, sea caves and green clad shore . . ."

Farther south along the coast is the town of Morro Bay, with scenic Morro Rock and three unlovely smokestacks. There is a popular pair of state parks in the area.

Salinas

Salinas, south of San Francisco and seat of Monterey County, was once the pasture land of the Carmel mission. Today, though it is a market center for vegetables and dairy produce, it is still a ranching area at heart. Fertile Salinas Valley is cattle country. Lettuce is very important in the bottom land, and also beets, grain, alfalfa, and berry patches. The Salinas Rodeo, in July, dates back to the time before California was a state. Salinas was John Steinbeck's home.

Fresno

Set in flat San Joaquin Valley, rimmed by vineyards, Fresno is just about midway between San Francisco and Los Angeles. Fresno (Spanish for "ash tree") was initially cattle country, and became a town after the gold rush, with the coming of the railway. The surrounding San Joaquin Valley has seasonal water from the Sierras. Controlled irrigation has helped in the growing of grapes. It is probably the raisin capital of the world. Nearby fig orchards are also important. Manufacturing contributes to the city's economy, with flour and lumber mills, soap factories, and brick works. Not far away are the Sierra National Forest, Sequoia National Forest, Sequoia National Park, and King's Canyon National Park.

The Lake and Mountain Country

"There is a love of wild nature in everybody, an ancient mother love ever showing itself whether recognized or not, and however covered by cares and duties." So John Muir wrote, and he also recognized that nowhere in the world can this love be better fulfilled than in California.

Mount Whitney, the highest point in the United States, is only sixty miles from Death Valley, the lowest area on the continent. Mount Whitney, 14,496 feet in altitude, is in the craggy southern Sierra. Yosemite National Park offers profound scenic refreshment in the midsection of the Sierra. Impressive clusters of the giant sequoia trees, largest living things, are found in the Giant Forest and Grant Grove in Sequoia and King's Canyon national parks east of the San Joaquin Valley.

Mammoth Lakes, on the opposite side of the Sierra, is a region of lakes and resorts beloved by fishermen and vacationers. This area of the rugged Sierra Nevada slopes was the scene of a gold rush in the 1870s. Pyramid Peak gives a view of thirty lakes, including Lake Tahoe.

Volcanos

In the Cascade Range in Miocene times, volcanos spewed forth a lava plateau which stretches all the way into Wyoming. There are remote spots on Mount Shasta, in Shasta National Forest, where steam still bubbles and hisses. Five glaciers hang from its flanks. Mount Shasta, one of the most dramatic sights in California, looms so high that it can be seen from a hundred miles away. Dormant volcano Mount Lassen, in Lassen National Park at the northern end of the Sierre Nevada, has deep snows in winter. In the Park are boiling lakes, steam vents, jagged cliffs, and lava-wrecked land.

Lake Tahoe

California and Nevada share Lake Tahoe, loveliest of lakes and deepest in the United States. It is near the crest of the Sierra and was formed by glaciers and faulting. Tahoe is an Indian name. The lake is 21.6 miles long and twelve miles wide.

A seventy-three-mile drive around Lake Tahoe offers a varied shoreline with cliffs, coves, sand beaches, garish resorts. This is a great vacation area, with meadows and heavily timbered slopes, and many modern campgrounds.

In the nearby Squaw Valley State Recreation area there are ski runs and facilities for winter sports. The Winter Olympic Games have been held here. There are three national forests in the area—Toiyabe on the Nevada side, Tahoe and Eldorado in California. Cascade Lake is one of the many small glacial lakes in the region of thick forests and craggy granite known as the Desolation Valley Wild Area.

SOUTHERN CALIFORNIA

Vastly different in terrain and style of life are Southern and Northern California. Once sabre-toothed tigers, the imperial elephant, giant wolves, camels, bison, and many smaller creatures roamed Los Angeles Basin. Evidence is found in fossils from the La Brea Pits in Los Angeles County, where pools of asphalt trapped prehistoric animals. The fossils are on display at the Los Angeles Museum of Natural History.

Los Angeles County has long been stamped with the glamor of the moviemakers. Disneyland is synonymous with delightful make-believe, drawing millions of visitors from all lands. Khrushchev was angry when he found that security precautions would not permit him to see Disneyland.

But the newest glamor in this part of the world is that of the jet and space age. Some of the first rocket and jet propulsion experiments were made at the California Institute of Technology—Caltech—in Pasadena, ten miles northeast of the city of Los Angeles. The Jet Propulsion Laboratory of Caltech now does major research on space travel and machinery for the National Aeronautics and Space Administration. Research and production of space-age hardware have charged Southern California with a new and potent stimulus. Missile and electronics manufacturing are attracting a new breed of highly trained scientists, engineers, and technicians.

The vitality of Southern California is forever being rejuvenated.

Los Angeles

Los Angeles, California's largest city, is a sprawling metropolis on the coast of California, 120 miles north of the Mexican border and 410 miles southeast of San Francisco.

From humble and unpretentious beginnings, it became officially in 1960 the third largest city in the United States. The population in 1940 was one and a half million; in the 1960 census 2,479,000, and with the influx of new residents at the rate of six hundred to a thousand a day, the figure is constantly rising. Comprising 458 square miles—which ranges from sea level to an altitude of more than 5,000 feet—Los Angeles is not a city in the accepted sense. Rather, it is an amalgamation of many related communities, each proud of its own traits and identity. The estimated population of the entire metropolitan Los Angeles area in 1968 was 8,455,000.

It is an area rich in agricultural bounty and in petroleum and is an enormous contributor to the fabulous industrial growth of the entire West Coast, particularly in aircraft and missile manufacturing and in the electronics industry.

Although the city was founded in 1781 by Governor Felipe de Neve, on a Spanish grant, and incorporated in 1850, its colorful history dates back much further. The Indian village near the site of the present city was called Yang-na. The first Spanish settlement was El Pueblo de Nuestra Señora la Reina de Los Angeles de Porciúncula (The Village of Our Lady, Queen of Angels).

Toward the beginning of the sixteenth century, explorers and adventurers from Portugal and Spain began to point the prows of their galleons toward discovery and conquest of the New World, some often touching the coast of California by accident on their return from the Orient, others stopping off to give much-needed rest and sustenance to their emaciated crews.

Los Angeles initially grew up around the famed Mission San Gabriel Arcángel, founded in 1771. Within thirty years hundreds of Indians had become drovers of thousands of head of cattle on vast ranches surrounding the mission. In 1822 came news of the Mexican revolution—the War of Independence of that country—and Mexico took over the government of Los Angeles as Spain relinquished her western possessions.

The stirring accomplishments of the Franciscan fathers in colonization, in converting the Indians, and in restraining the savage instincts of the conquerors have few parallels in history. Despite the beauty of their buildings, their wealth and gardens, and the fact that they were producing 123,000 bushels of grain, tending almost 880,000 head of cattle and other livestock, and cultivating orchards and vineyards, the Missions, upon secularization enforced by the Mexican government in 1834, were destroyed or permitted to decay from planned neglect.

Americans from the East soon began to filter into the area—some by sea, others by land. Within a few years the Yankees had become large land owners and were exercising control of the area's trade and commerce. They grew so powerful that they began to be viewed as a menace to the peace and security of Mexico and were tagged with the label "foreign agitators." Many Americans and some Englishmen were arrested, tried and deported in chains to Mexico. The events that followed could lead down only one path—to war. The United States, under the slogan of "Manifest Destiny," wanted its union to extend from the Atlantic to the Pacific.

Many skirmishes and battles ensued. Finally the United States forces, under General S. W. Kearny and Commodore R. I. Stockton, defeated the Mexicans.

It remained for Captain John C. Frémont to secure the formal capitulation of the Mexican forces under command of General Andrés Picó, on January 13, 1847. When California was admitted to the Union in 1850, the first United States census of that year listed the newly incorporated village of Los Angeles with a population of 1,610 inhabitants.

The discovery of gold in northern California in 1848 had an ill effect on the village, at the outset, luring many Angelenos away from their pueblos to seek their fortunes. But before long, new immigrants began to pour into the area and create a new wave of prosperity. There was also the lure of another ore—silver—discovered in the town of Calico, so named because of the colorful mountains surrounding it. During the period from 1881 to 1896, mining activities produced between 67 and 86 million dollars in silver. But soon the price of the metal dropped, and the town and its mines were abandoned and left to ruin.

Until 1876 the only transportation between Los Angeles and its neighboring states was by sea, stagecoach, or wagon train. That year marked the advent of the "Iron Horse," when the Southern Pacific Railroad expanded its service from San Francisco south to Los Angeles. In 1885, after a surprising and phenomenal land boom, another railroad became a serious competitor when the Santa Fe Railway completed its line to Los Angeles. Still another was the Union Pacific Railroad, originally incorporated and approved by President Lincoln in 1862 as a war measure. The Union Pacific was a part of the first transcontinental railroad.

An ensuing rate war stimulated Easterners into moving west for the climate or for profit, being intrigued by a revival of the gold-rush fever, and the railroads attracted new and large populations into settling in the area.

Hordes of people flocked to the city, and the resultant rise in land values seemed at first only a natural outcome. Before long, prices of land in and around Los Angeles mushroomed out of control. Sanity was eventually restored and the boom properly deflated except for land referred to as "downtown property." A new stimulus to the entire region occurred in 1860 with the discovery of oil in the Newhall-Ventura district. Promoters seized upon this fabulous eruption of "black gold" and, in a short space of time, about 3,000 wells had been drilled. The first drilling within the city limits of that day was done in 1892, and soon rigs and derricks were as close as corn stalks. California was soon producing one fourth of the world's petroleum supply, most of it from Los Angeles county.

Another important contributor to the growth of the Los Angeles region was, and still is, agriculture, particularly the citrus industry. The first orange grove was planted about 1805, and today orange production is highly developed and carefully inspected and regulated. It reached a peak in the early 1950s, California's 330,000 acres then producing approximately 60 per cent of all the oranges grown in the United States—more than fifty million crates a year—and almost 100 per cent of its lemons. Agriculture in California today takes second place only to manufacturing.

To market citrus produce, a nonprofit, cooperative agency was formed. The development of oranges and orange juice as breakfast items and the promotion of the benefits of vitamin C is history. Frozen orange-juice concentrate has been the most recent boon to the industry.

An important adjunct to the growth of Los Angeles was the construction of a deep-water harbor at San Pedro, the largest man-made harbor in the world, developed from a dismal flat. It is estimated that today ships carry annually more than twenty-four million tons of cargo through this port.

Indeed, the Pacific Ocean has played an important role in attracting people from all over the world to this city of Our Lady. From the time of the early explorers to the time of the present-day surfing enthusiast, the high-crested waves of the vast and alluring Pacific have been legend, and the beaches around Los Angeles have been havens for pleasure seekers.

On the other hand, the supply of fresh water was a sore problem for years. For well over a century the sometimes Los Angeles River was the only source of water for the town, but it could supply water for only a quarter of a million residents. Under the direction of William Mulholland, plans were drawn for the construction of an aqueduct that could deliver enough water for two million people. The source was the Owens River and its tributaries three hundred miles northeast, fed by the snow waters of the Sierra Nevada. Upon completion, the system comprised 142 separate tunnels totaling fifty-three miles in length, twelve miles of inverted steel siphons, twenty-four miles of open unlined conduit, thirty-nine miles of open cement-lined conduit, and ninety-seven miles of covered conduit. Three great reservoirs took up another several miles, the largest of which was the Haiwee Reservoir, with a storage capacity of nineteen million gallons of water. The people of the Owens Valley fought the siphoning off of their water.

Perhaps there were many reasons why the motion-picture industry came to Hollywood, a part of Los Angeles. The industry's origins were in the East, where Vitagraph and other studios pioneered on Long Island. But whatever other reasons there may have been, the mild climate was the chief attraction, conducive to the construction of lots and sets that recaptured another adventuresome period of the Golden West.

With some misgivings, great courage, and unlimited vision came the industry's pioneers, as far back as 1909. Hollywood, despite periodic tribulations, is today the cinema capital of the world, a magnet for stars and starlets, greats and near greats, and their admirers. Films are distributed worldwide. More than a score of independent studios are engaged largely in the production of television films.

Los Angeles has never really lost its Spanish flavor. A modified Spanish colonial style of architecture was for years the predominant motif in housing and public buildings. The old town's central plaza still remains, along with the Mexican shops of Olvera Street, the stucco or adobe walls, the barred windows, grilled balconies, and Spanish-type patios. Gardens grow in semi-tropical brilliance, with bougainvillea, Cup of Gold, wistaria, hibiscus, and poinsettia. Orange blossoms perfume the air. By winter, from the sun-drenched Los Angeles plain one can look out to nearby snow-capped mountain peaks. As a matter of fact, Los Angeles County contains a great variety of geography, landscape, and climate. Excellent roads make it possible to go from ocean beach to ski slopes in a few hours—barring traffic.

So publicized are the crowded freeways, the antics of Hollywood stars, the weird quasi-religious cults, the fantastic maze of Disneyland, and the ballyhoo and tinsel of the movie industry, that one has a tendency to overlook the fact that millions of Angelenos live completely normal lives, working in factory and office, returning home every evening to barbecue the family dinner, watch television, and enjoy an occasional visit to the movies, theater, concert, or restaurant. The great majority of the population lives in complete oblivion to the peculiar exhibitionism of a few or the blatant claims of publicity men.

Among the delights of Los Angeles are its new Music Center (a complex of three modern and well-appointed theaters) and the following: an outstanding public library system . . . a county art museum of importance . . . an assortment of parks, hillside, and seaside . . . a new zoo with obvious shortcomings but still a joy to small children . . . a pair of downtown museums—one featuring science and industry, the other natural-history objects . . . the noted University of Southern California and a galaxy of smaller, excellent private colleges . . . a restaurant "row"—La Cienega Boulevard—that rivals San Francisco or New York. (Los Angeles has improved dramatically as a fine town in which to dine in postwar years.) There are ball parks, stadia, sports arenas, and playing fields for every known domestic sport. TV and radio stations still bid visitors welcome. An observatory explains the mysteries of the stars, while those who are interested in human stars can purchase maps to the celebrities' homes on many streetcorners. The Greater Los Angeles region has an alligator farm, a Jungleland complex, a Japanese deer park, a celebrity wax museum, a museum devoted to classic automobiles, one for old airplanes, and a display of sabre-toothed tigers.

The core of the sprawling metropolis after World War II developed some symptoms of decline. Today downtown Los Angeles is being rejuvenated in a burst of gleaming towers. Though the central city has always remained the region's stronghold for banking, finance, oil, and insurance, other industries and their jobs had begun to follow the people to the suburbs. Streets once bustling were becoming depressed areas. The skyline was never exhilarating, because fear of earthquakes set low ceilings on vertical growth. Los Angeles spread horizontally. Until 1959 a local ordinance limited buildings to a height of thirteen stories or 150 feet. That ceiling has been abolished, and a new, handsome, and higher skyline is being built.

In the first eight years of the 1960s businessmen committed eight hundred million dollars for downtown building and remodeling. By 1970, investment in this decade yielded nine million square feet of new office space, almost twice as much as was built downtown in the first sixty years of the century. A forty-two-story headquarters and office building of the Crocker-Citizens National Bank, opened in 1968, is the tallest structure in the city. Plans were announced by the Bank of America and Atlantic Richfield Company for a $140,000,000 office-and-shopping-center complex that will be forty-seven feet higher, with fifty-two-story towers rising 667 feet above a land-scaped mall. The sprouting skyline is now beginning to match Los Angeles aspirations toward being a commercial and cultural center of the West. Most of the new skyscrapers have sprung up along the sector of the freeway loop that is closest to the downtown core. Land prices have increased as much as 500 per cent in five years. There is even a reviving demand for walk-to-work living in this city—so wedded to the automobile—and lofty apartments are rising to meet it.

Hollywood

Incorporated as a village in 1903, Hollywood surrendered its charter in 1910 to become a part of Los Angeles. Movie stars and many of the studios have long since moved out of Hollywood, which is now a business community and home of the average family. Today the studios are scattered over a wide area that includes both Hollywood and neighboring cities—Burbank, Universal City, and Culver City. Sunset Strip, once lined with exclusive restaurants, cabarets, and specialty shops, has faded. Hollywood lives on, however, as a state of mind and spirit that stirred the great masses of the American people from their provincial restraint and attracted vast numbers of people to leave the chilly North or dusty Midwest to come to Southern California's idealized shores. In Hollywood, Grauman's Chinese theater is still the place where super premieres are staged amid a battery of floodlights, and motion-picture celebrities may be seen at such events. The pavement in the forecourt of the theater has the foot and hand prints and the signatures of stars cast in the concrete. Hollywood Bowl is set in a natural amphitheater in the chaparral-covered hills. It seats 20,000 for concerts, operas, ballets, and pageants.

Beverly Hills

Sunset Boulevard, which starts at the ocean's edge, passes through Beverly Hills and Hollywood, with side streets leading to the exclusive residential districts of Bel Air, Brentwood, and Westwood Hills. Beverly Hills, a smaller independent city, is surrounded by Los Angeles. Laid out in 1907, it is still home to many famous movie stars, though others have built further afield. The hotels here are as luxurious as the homes. Wilshire Boulevard in Beverly Hills is Los Angeles' Fifth Avenue, a truly exclusive shopping area referred to as the Miracle Mile. The University of California in Los Angeles (UCLA) is in Westwood Hills.

Santa Monica

One of Los Angeles' most popular coastal suburbs is the residential and resort community of Santa Monica, with one of the best beaches of white sand curving beside the sheltered waters of Santa Monica Bay. The city of Santa Monica commands the cliffs above the Pacific.

Long Beach

Long Beach, the area's second-largest city, is another magnetic attraction. Nearby is a great man-made harbor and one of the state's most productive oil fields. It is a favorite with retired midwesterners, who enjoy the cool ocean breezes, the eight-mile stretch of beach, and the extensive recreation program for the elderly. Hundreds of oil derricks stand on the crest of Signal Hill overlooking the city. Shipping is one of the major factors in the city's economy, for this is the fifth-largest port in the state. Long Beach is closely connected with developing Wilmington, which has a major underwater oil reserve. The manufacture of aircraft and the production of chemicals are important industries in Long Beach and Wilmington. There is a large naval shipyard here.

Inglewood

Inglewood is a residential and industrial community just south of Los Angeles. The Adobe Del Rancho Aguaje de la Centinela is all that remains of the Spanish past. Here is Hollywood Park, the ultramodern home of thoroughbreds during Southern California's summer racing season.

Palos Verdes

Palos Verdes is a handsome residential district of predominantly Mediterranean style. Nearby is the slim white tower of Point Vicente Lighthouse. On Palos Verdes Drive South, beside the sea, is Marineland of the Pacific, a three-ring sea circus where whales, dolphins, and sea lions cavort and stage delightful shows. Thousands of colorful fishes swim serenely behind viewing windows.

Newport Beach

Newport Beach on Newport Bay is a fast-growing ocean-oriented recreation area. The boat harbor, dredged in 1872, is spacious. Here in the spring the Pacific Coast Regatta is held, and in the summer the Tournament of Lights, a water carnival.

Nearby, three miles in from the ocean, is the University of California—Irvine, which opened in 1966. It is one of the recent fine examples of how the state's university system responds and expands to meet the needs of the growing rush of students to the colleges.

Pasadena

Pasadena is ten miles northeast of Los Angeles, against the San Gabriel Mountain foothills. The stately city is tree-shaded and a center of electronics and precision-instruments manufacturing. It is the retail trade center for the San Gabriel Valley. The city is also the home of the Rose Bowl, the California Institute of Technology (Caltech), and the Pasadena College of Theatrical Arts. The Rose Bowl, home of the Rose Bowl football game on New Year's Day, seats 85,000 people. Caltech has long been famous for the work of its distinguished physicists and other scientific research. Here are found the W. K. Kellogg Radiation Laboratory, Firestone Flight Science Laboratory, Guggenheim Graduate School of Aeronautics, Karman Laboratory of Flight Mechanics and Jet Propulsion, and the Willis H. Booth Computing Center.

San Fernando Valley

East of the Santa Monica Mountains is the flat plain of the San Fernando Valley, where more than a million people reside. Very popular with retired people of moderate income, the area also encloses such luxurious neighborhoods as Encino and Sherman Oaks.

San Gabriel Mountains

A number of delightful residential communities other than Pasadena ring the base of the San Gabriel Mountains. Altadena, Azusa, Glendora, and Sierra Madre all have a mountain background. Six miles northwest of Pasadena, at the base of the mountains, is the community of La Canada, home of the Descanso Gardens. Roses, azaleas, orchids, begonias, and many other blooming plants make this a delightful mecca for flower lovers.

Knott's Berry Farm and Ghost Town

South of Los Angeles, near the town of Buena Park on U.S. 101, in a region of truck gardens, citrus groves, and oil fields, the Knott family planted a berry farm in the 1920s. They made berry pies and berry jam and offered chicken dinners. In the 1940s they produced ghosts, and prospered. The Ghost Town is a nostalgic reincarnation of the days of high adventure and violence in the Old West. The buildings, their furnishings, the entertainment, and the shows are designed to conjure up the spirit of '49.

Disneyland

Anaheim, about twenty-eight miles southeast of Los Angeles, was a pleasant town surrounded by orange groves when Walt Disney built Disneyland in 1955. Today Disneyland draws millions of visitors from all over the world. Each Disneyland visitor brings away with him a different set of memories of this magical world. Skeptical travelers who come prepared to be a little dubious about it all quickly succumb, for Disneyland is probably the world's greatest man-made attraction. Happy adult visitors outnumber children about four to one.

Main Street is a distillation of nostalgia, rolling back the years to the 1890s. The Jungle River Boat cruise is wildly exciting, with the bright river boat chugging down narrow waterways swarming with hippopotami and elephants taking a bath. Many travelers repeat the trip several times . . . and there is much more.

The best way to get an idea of all that there is to see and do is to ride the monorail and get an eye-popping view of the wonders below. The Santa Fe Disneyland Railroad makes a circle get-acquainted tour. Guided tours are recommended for a visitor who has never been there, and the happy young guides are as much fun as the Fantasyland they take you through. It is possible to spend several enthralled days here before you see it all.

Laguna Beach

Laguna Beach is a delightful resort beloved by artists on the shore south of Long Beach. It draws thousands to its annual cultural events, including the festival of arts, festival of opera, and civic ballet. A theater, a chamber music society, and many art galleries grace the city.

San Diego

California history began at San Diego, which has one of the finest natural harbors in the world. There, the first of the famous chain of Spanish missions was built in colonial days. San Diego has enjoyed a leisurely life as a Spanish and Mexican pueblo, an American town, and later an important naval base. The arrival of the missile and aircraft industries in the area, and the attractions of its mild and perennially sunny climate brought about a spectacular growth.

The bay is a haven for U.S. Navy ships, merchant vessels, and private boats of every description. The life of the city, economic and recreational, centers upon this great bay, sheltered from storms by the bluffs of Point Loma. The U.S. Navy and Marine Corps have vast permanent shore establishments around the city. Most residents and visitors live on the beaches, sailing, diving, lazing in the kind sun, and enjoying the splendid water vacationland.

Balboa Park, in the middle of the city, is famous for its fourteen hundred acres of pastoral beauty, its excellent zoo, the Fine Arts Gallery blessed with a collection of Spanish paintings by El Greco, Murillo, Zurbarán, Goya, Sorolla, and Zuloaga, and the San Diego Museum of Man, which houses a collection of Mayan, Aztec, and Indian artifacts. Those who know zoos consider San Diego's one of the world's finest. It has the world's largest collection of animals—more than four thousand—and they are housed beautifully and imaginatively. Sea World in San Diego is a splendid marine aquarium, complete with a killer whale.

The cradle of Spanish California is at Presidio Park, atop a hill overlooking Old Town. The Old Town Spanish Plaza is the noteworthy feature of downtown San Diego. The city's cultural life is a source of pride, and art galleries, music festivals, and drama have prospered here.

The so-called "Old Spanish Lighthouse"—which isn't Spanish but is old—is perched on the south end of Point Loma, breakwater for the bay, and gives a great view of the city and the shore. It is now Cabrillo National Monument. Whale-watching is a favorite sport from this vantage point when the gray whales migrate past, just offshore, during winter months.

La Jolla is a delightful residential and resort area of San Diego, about five miles north of Mission Bay. Here is the famed Scripps Institution of Oceanography, with a museum and aquarium. Farther north on the coast is Torrey Pinas Mesa, part of which is a state park. It is the only spot in America where the rangy, twisted Torrey pine grows. Here also sailplane buffs meet weekly and sailplanes cruise gracefully from a gliderport over the coast.

San Diego also provides easy access to the vacationland of Mexico. Seventeen miles south of the city is the international border at Tijuana, Mexiko, where bullfights, jai-alai games, and attractive Mexican shops court tourists.

The rich agricultural areas of San Diego to the east rank high among the nation's counties in total production and lead in growing avocados, in spite of a periodic water shortage.

Coronado, on the opposite point of a peninsula from San Diego on San Diego Bay, is a peaceful resort with beautiful houses and a great enthusiasm for water sports.

The San Diego back country lures the explorer by automobile with quiet valleys, wooded mountains, fine state parks, lovely lakes, and attractive desert area. The mountains of the county begin at the seashore, rise gradually toward the east, and then drop abruptly to the desert. Indian reservations such as the Pechanga, Pauma, La Jolla, Santa Isabel, and Viejas have interesting mission churches and chapels seldom seen by the public.

San Diego's Back Country

Northeast of San Diego, atop Mount Palomar, the Palomar observatory dome houses the 200-inch Hale telescope, largest in the world. Operated by the California Institute of Technology, the observatory has unraveled many riddles of outer space. Visitors can tour the observatory, which is open to the public daily.

East of San Diego's central mountain range, adjacent to the Imperial Valley, stretches a half million acres of desert wilderness, in which is situated the Anza-Borrego Desert State Park. This is a brilliant world for the confirmed desert lover. Hunting is prohibited, and patient visitors may spot a desert bighorn ram, or perhaps coyotes, bobcats, or ringtail cats. The park offers fine camping facilities.

Interesting is the Salton Sea, between the rich farmlands of the Imperial and Coachella valleys. The present lake was formed in 1905, when the Colorado River overflowed and its flood waters were caught in the basin. Rock hunters love the deep, colorful side canyons. Powerboat racers consider the sea a very fast body of water. Boats may be rented beside the sea, and there is camping at Salton Sea State Park.

The dry Imperial Valley is irrigated by water diverted from the Colorado River and impounded at Imperial Dam, in one of the most massive irrigation projects in the world. The water has made the fertile acres vastly productive, with excellent crops of cantaloupes, head lettuce, and alfalfa, used for highly developed cattle-feeding operations.

Ventura

Several attractive cities are perched along the shore northwest of Los Angeles, beside the Santa Barbara Channel. Ventura, a growing coastal resort, is sixty-two miles northwest of Los Angeles. It is an exporting center for oil and farm produce—vegetables, walnuts, fruit, and beef cattle. To the east is Santa Clara Valley, a fertile strip sheltered by the San Rafael Range on the north. The valley also produces oil, discovered here in 1866, and is still producing though it is the oldest oil field to be tapped in California.

Santa Barbara

About ninety miles northeast of Los Angeles, on the curving coast that fronts on Santa Barbara Channel, is the city of Santa Barbara, one of the most attractive in California. The traditional architecture, beautiful gardens and patios, old adobes, and mission retain the flavor of Spanish days. Vizcaíno named the region when he sailed into the channel on Saint Barbara's Day, December 4, 1603. Captain José Francisco Ortega founded the presidio here in 1782, and the mission was established in 1786. The Barbareños, many of them "dons" bearing noble names, raised cattle on vast acreage and enjoyed a gracious and hospitable life.

The city lies on a coastal shelf that rises into the southern slopes of the Santa Ynez Mountains. About it all is an air of spaciousness, wealth, and quiet comfort. Many of its business buildings harmonize with the Spanish style. The Court House is one of the best examples of Spanish-Moorish architecture in America. Mission Santa Bárbara, Queen of the Missions, is considered to be the most attractive and best preserved of the twenty-one missions.

A wide, gently curving beach spreads beside the channel. The beauty of the waterfront has been carefully preserved, and the eastern end of the beach is a bird refuge. Oil drilling within the city and in the ocean opposite the city has been forbidden. Offshore oil drilling platforms contribute to the economy of the area but have caused problems.

Santa Barbara's famous Moreton Bay fig tree (*Ficus macraphylla*) has a circumference of 29 feet and covers an estimated area of 12,000 square feet. This import from Australia provides no edible fruit, but it is said that 9,500 people can stand in its shade at noon. Santa Barbara folks love their famous fig tree.

Scenic hillside drives behind the town offer magnificent views. The Los Padres National Forest stretches to the north and south behind the city.

San Luis Obispo

San Luis Obispo fronts the open Pacific about two hundred miles northwest of Los Angeles. To the north rise the Santa Lucia Mountains. Indians were friendly here when Father Serra landed to establish a mission, because soldiers of the Portolá expedition in 1772 had killed several of the great bears that were marauding in the area. California State Polytechnic College is in San Luis Obispo.

The Channel Islands

Two groups of islands lie off the coast of California. There are the nine Channel Islands, which are strung from Point Conception almost to San Diego, lying twenty to sixty miles offshore. From San Clemente Island in the south to San Miguel Island in the north, the distance is 155 miles. Near San Francisco are the Farallones, a group of six small rocky islands about twenty-eight miles west of the entrance to San Francisco Bay. The Farallon Islands are a bird refuge and are topped by a lighthouse that is one of the most powerful on the coast.

Santa Catalina Island

Santa Catalina Island is separated by the San Pedro Channel from Long Beach and Wilmington, twenty-seven miles away to the northeast on the mainland. This is the largest and most important of the Channel Islands. Catalina is twenty miles long and from eight miles to one-half mile wide. From the mainland it looks like a drowned mountain top. Foliage is luxuriant in its many valleys, and the rugged higher slopes are rather barren.

Juan Rodriguez Cabrillo discovered the island in 1543. It is named for St. Catherine. Russians landed in the bay early in the nineteenth century, slaughtering sea lions and Indians. The island had a gold rush following a rich strike in 1863. Then came a pirate scare during the Civil War, and then the gold ran out.

William Wrigley, Jr., who bought Santa Catalina in 1919, spent a fortune in creating Avalon, a romantic palm-studded town on the bay, where he is buried. It was he who made it a successful resort and tourist attraction. Avalon is refreshing, with the shade of palms and olive trees, grassy squares, and sparkling fountains. On occasions, costumed señoritas in spangles and strumming troubadours in velvet set the tone of the scene. The Avalon Casino is on the boardwalk.

Eagles nest on the thousand-foot peak of Eagle Mountain. Hunting is a rugged sport here. Boars and wild mountain goats, but not the eagles, are hunted the year round from horseback. Fishing is fine, with many tuna, swordfish, yellowtail, white sea bass, rock bass, barracuda, mackerel, bonita, whitefish, and sheepshead found in waters round the island. Glass-bottom-boat trips allow the visitor to see marine gardens on the north shore, and there is a cruise to a cluster of rocks nearby, where several hundred sea lions live.

Santa Catalina Island can be reached by water taxi from several mainland points and by seaplane from at least three Southland airports. The old Big White Steamer is no more. Catalina's biggest business is still tourism.

Channel Islands National Monument

Two of the Channel Islands, Anacapa and Santa Barbara, offshore from San Pedro, form the Channel Islands National Monument and are administered by the National Park Service. Haunted by sea lions, the islands are visited occasionally by the huge sea elephant and the Guadalupe fur seal. The giant coreopsis blooms in such profusion in the spring that it can be seen miles away.

San Bernardino

East of Los Angeles lies San Bernardino, county seat of San Bernardino County and a gateway to the vast San Bernardino National Forest. The first American settlers in the town were five hundred Mormons from Salt Lake City who laid out a city here in 1852. They were recalled by Brigham Young in 1857. It is the site of Norton Air Force Base, one of the largest in the Southwest, and of San Bernardino Valley College.

In the San Bernardino and San Jacinto Mountains are many attractive resorts with rustic lodges and cabins. Forest fires are a hazard in the dry season.

Bakersfield

Bakersfield, at the southern end of San Joaquin Valley, is blessed by the riches of the region around it, which produces livestock and poultry, grapes and wine, and oil and natural gas. The ranches are checkerboarded between various oil fields. Gold was found high in the Kern River Canyon in 1885, and Bakersfield became a rough and tough boom town. The old mountain camp of Whiskey Flat became the town of Isabella when it became prosperous.

The discovery of oil in 1899 brought another wild boom. Many motion-picture companies have produced westerns around here. It is 110 miles from Bakersfield to Los Angeles over a super-lative mountain highway that climbs through Grapevine Canyon in the Tehachapi Range, and passes old Fort Tejon.

Palm Springs

Beyond the San Jacinto Mountains, east of Los Angeles, lie Palm Springs and Indio and the rich Coachella Valley, date capital of the United States. Palm Springs is one of the most fashion-able winter resort towns in the West. Elegant homes, eighteen golf courses, and 3,350 swimming pools ameliorate life here. It is an ultrasmart playground for industrialists as well as movie stars.

The locale was first known as Agua Caliente, because of its hot springs. The sleepy little town on a shelf of the San Jacinto Mountains at the edge of the desert became a favored resort in the 1930s, when a highway was cut through the mountains to Los Angeles. A marvelous ride up the side of the mountain now is provided by the Palm Springs Aerial Tramway, which starts near the town and soars, over cliffs and chasms, for two and a half miles to a mountain station 8,516 feet up on a flank of Mount San Jacinto. There is a restaurant and chalet at the end of the ride. San Jacinto Peak can be seen for a hundred miles.

Indio

Indio is the distribution and trade center for the Coachella Valley, where grapes, dates, and citrus are the important crops. The dates, imported and planted in 1904, are delicious and may be bought at many roadside stands.

THE HIGH MOUNTAINS AND THE DESERTS

More and more, sophisticated Californians turn for recreation to the high back country, the forbidding mountains, and the brilliant deserts over which the pioneers plodded. They explore abandoned quarries, take the side roads, find opals, dig for fossils. There are many rockhounds.

Old mines and ghost towns lure them. Mountain climbing induces them to forget trivia. They discover the fantastic beauty of the California deserts when the rains come, and how cold a desert night can be. They plunge into the ice-cooled waters of blue mountain lakes. They may hunt or fish, but largely they relish what is wild and lonely. In no place can people do all this more comfortably than in California, with its many convenient campsites.

One of the joyous things about the Los Angeles area is that so much wild country stands close at hand.

The Santa Monica Mountains still know the tracks of coyote and bobcat and places where Indians have made meal of acorns and sites where fossils can be tooled from the old stones.

Humpbacked along the east-west sky are the San Gabriel Mountains, the realm of the Angeles National Forest, one of the first in the nation. A great ridge-following highway travels much of this mountain-high country—the Angeles Crest Highway. Along its span is the astronomical outpost of famed Mount Wilson, timbered campgrounds, ski resorts, picnic grounds patrolled by gray squirrels. In the wilderness regions here hide bighorn sheep, mountain lions, black bear.

Within two hours from downtown Los Angeles it is possible to be swallowed in the pine forests of the San Gabriels.

Farther east are the San Bernardino Mountains—and the San Bernardino National Forest. Here are the mile-high resorts of Crestline, Lake Arrowhead, Big Bear, Barton Flats. There is rugged country here—to scale Mount San Gorgonio is to climb Southern California's tallest peak, two miles high.

Rising above Palm Springs on the desert floor is Mount San Jacinto. A tramway to its summit affords a magnificent view to the east of the Joshua Tree National Monument and the Mojave and Colorado Deserts. On exceptionally clear days one can see distant mountains across the Colorado River in Arizona.

Mount Whitney

Mount Whitney (14,495 ft.), the tallest peak in the continental United States, can be approached from the east or from the west. It is a nine-day trip from the west, three days from the east. The approach from the west is from Mineral King or Crescent Meadow. Mount Whitney rises from the eastern edge of Sequoia National Park. The approach from the east follows Lone Pine Creek and deadends at the trail that leads to the top of the peak. The town of Lone Pine, on Highway 395, specializes in outfitting hikers for trips to Mount Whitney's summit. The mighty peak was named in honor of Professor J. D. Whitney, leader of the survey party that in 1864 determined that this was the highest peak in the United States, exclusive of Alaska. The trail from the east climbs six thousand feet in thirteen miles. It is at the very least a two-day hike.

Though you may decide against the climb to the top, there is much fascinating scenery in the general area, such as the Alabama Hills, great weird masses of granite. In the Inyo National Forest there is a splendid four-mile hiking trail up to Kearsarge Pass from Onion Valley.

Highway 395 parallels the Owens River in Owens Valley, a long and narrow trough between the two-mile-high ridge of the Sierra Nevada to the west and the equally high Inyo and White Mountain chain to the east. It leads into the most dramatic stretch of the cool Sierra. There are ghost towns such as Cerro Gordo in the mountain mining country on the northeast shore of Owens Lake, and sleepy Keeler, where miners once roared in rows of saloons when silver started coming out of the Inyo Mountains.

Panamint Country

Lonely Panamint Valley, bounded by the Panamint Range to the east and the Argus and Inyo ranges to the west, has preserved the flavor of the Old West. There are miners' markings along the trails. Wild horses hide in the hills. From Panamint Springs, east of Lone Pine, experienced desert drivers can make trips to many an abandoned mine.

Death Valley

Two well-traveled highways run through Death Valley, east and west, and north and south. They are well patrolled by the rangers of Death Valley National Monument. There are improved camp grounds. The fantastic desert scenery can be enjoyed quite comfortably from the highways. Dirt roads branch off to sites such as the vanished ghost town of Skidoo. At Grapevine Junction a road leads to Scotty's Castle, the huge mansion of "Death Valley Scotty."

Mojave Desert

The Mojave Desert is known for the crossing of the twenty-mule teams out of Death Valley, for Edwards Air Force Base, where strange rocket craft are tested, and for the riches of yesterday's mines at Randsburg and Johannesburg and Red Mountain. Here the Naval Weapons Center at China Lake and the finest canyon of ancient Indian rock writing in the desert region are only a few miles apart.

There are ghost towns and vanished towns and old mine headframes and awesome shafts in the ground. There are Indian arrowheads and fossils and gemstones for the hardy seekers. There are a thousand miles of jeep roads and by spring and summer, a world of infinitesimal wildflowers—here called belly flowers—that corral every color in the Western rainbow.

The desert has water, if you know where to look; and the camps of Ute horse thieves who once robbed the Spanish, and the crossing places of the Mormon emigrants and the Death Valley survivors.

Camels crossed the California desert country, but now the Mojave is etched by superhighways. The lonesome places between the highways hold the delicious secrets of the unknown Mojave Desert.

Joshua Tree National Monument

The spacious Joshua Tree National Monument is the high desert at its wildest. Because its lowest level is three to four thousand feet in altitude, it is seldom too hot, even in summer. Exotic are the strange Joshua trees. Junipers and piñon pines sing in the wind in the canyons. The weird wonderland of rock and trees has eight public campgrounds.

NATIONAL PARKS AND MONUMENTS

Yosemite National Park

As the world shrinks and population burgeons, so do our natural retreats diminish in size and number—and increase enormously in value and importance. Widely recognized today, this concept was radical and visionary in the 1860s when John Muir, one of America's great naturalists and founder of the Sierra Club, began his unceasing efforts that secured Yosemite for the inspiration and enjoyment of all.

Although authorship was secondary for John Muir, almost incidental to his career as mountaineer, explorer, and student of nature, his power to evoke the awesome majesty of the Sierra and Yosemite has never been equaled: "Looking eastward from the summit of the Pacheco Pass one shining morning," he wrote, "a landscape was displayed that after all my wanderings still appears as the most beautiful I have ever beheld. At my feet lay the Great Central Valley of California, level and flowery, like a lake of pure sunshine, forty or fifty miles wide, five hundred miles long, one rich furred garden of yellow *Compositae*. And from the eastern boundary of this vast golden flower bed rose the mighty Sierra, miles in height and so gloriously colored and so radiant, it seemed not clothed with light, but wholly composed of it, like the wall of some celestial city. ... Then it seemed to me that the Sierra should be called, not the Nevada or Snowy Range, but the Range of Light. And after ten years of wandering and wondering in the heart of it, rejoicing in its glorious floods of light, the white beams of the morning streaming through the passes, the noonday radiance on the crystal rocks, the flush of the alpenglow, and the irised spray of countless waterfalls, it still seems above all others the Range of Light."

Muir lived in Yosemite almost continuously from 1868 to 1873, contributing accurate and highly respected observations in geology and glaciology. These and subsequent years spent in his beloved Yosemite fostered Muir's passionate conservation campaigns and eventually led to the establishment of Federal Forest Reserves, and Yosemite Sequoia National Parks, and aided in the development of the National Park System.

Geologists and scientists, together with the average visitor, agree that the Yosemite Valley comprises one of the most fascinating and impressive geological formations on earth. For decades, experts were in sharp disagreement on the origin of Yosemite. Some contended that the beginning

116

was actually a great cataclysm and the consequent down-faulting of a large mass of granite; others, that a great earthquake had formed the valley. John Muir's own theory, that the valley had been created largely by glacial action, was roundly and scathingly denounced. The battle of the theories raged on until finally, in 1913, a United States Geological Survey group was sent into the area to resolve the question. Eventually (although too late for Muir to enjoy the vindication of his theory) it was determined that Yosemite had indeed been carved by the combined action of glaciers and the Merced River.

Yosemite National Park is situated about 150 miles due east of San Francisco in the rugged heart of the Sierra Nevada range. It is accessible from the north by Manteca's State Highway 120—from the south by State Highway 21 from Fresno. The park itself encompasses more than 750,000 acres on unbelievably beautiful wild terrain, vast forests, countless lakes, the watersheds of great rivers and awesome snow-crested peaks reaching skyward over 13,000 feet.

Many hundreds of varieties of animals, birds, trees, and shrubs thrive in the sequestered stronghold of Yosemite — and the giant sequoias tower over all. Three groves of these stupendous trees—the Merced, Tuolumne, and Mariposa—dominate their surrounds within the park. Yosemite must be seen and explored to be believed; no description or legend can offer more than a simple blaze mark to serve as a guide to its splendors. The lover of nature must see for himself the towering granite of El Capitan, the shimmering beauty of Bridal Veil Falls, and the placid valleys preserved for all and forever in Yosemite—John Muir's "mighty Sierra . . . so gloriously colored and so radiant, it seemed not clothed with light but wholly composed of it, like the wall of some celestial city."

Sequoia and Kings Canyon National Parks

Two of the great National Parks of California are linked, though by no means are they Siamese twins. They are Sequoia and Kings Canyon, high in the Sierra Nevada east of San Joaquin Valley.

The giant sequoias (*Sequoia gigantea*) loom here, their trunks the hue of rose-red brick. Men and women come here to be dwarfed. Here bear and coyotes roam. The trees are the largest living things on earth. The General Sherman, most massive of the giants in the Giant Forest, towers 272.4 feet. The General Grant tree is 267.4 feet in height. General Grant is fatter, with a circumference of 107.6 feet compared to Sherman's 101.6 feet. Climb Alta Peak and you can see a world of mountains. You will know why the range is called the Sierra Nevada, the Snowy Range. The big trees are native to a four-thousand-to-eight-thousand-foot zone in the western Sierra. The largest living specimens are thought to be about three thousand years old. The bark is one to two feet thick, fluted like Doric columns.

The Giant Forest was deeded to the United States in 1916, purchased with funds raised by the National Geographic Society and voted by the U.S. Congress. Kings Canyon, eight thousand feet deep, is the deepest in the continent, and here, in addition to the world's most massive trees, is the highest mountain in the continental United States, Mount Whitney. The place names are evocative—Black Giant, Grouse Meadows, Le Conte Canyon, Lake of the Fallen

Moon, Bearpaw Meadow. Here you can catch golden trout while golden eagles soar above you under a peak called Angel's Wings. The two parks, covering 1,322 square miles, are in the wildest country on the western slopes of the Sierra Nevada. A rough granite ridge, the Great Western Divide, bisects Sequoia National Park and is paralleled by the Kern River Canyon.

The region was first inhabited by the Yokut Indians.

The General Sherman Tree was named in 1879 by James Wolverton, a trapper, for his commander in the Civil War. In 1884 the Kaweah Colony, a socialistic group, came to build a Utopia in the wilderness. They named the giant trees after heroes of the French revolution. The General Sherman Tree was called the Karl Marx Tree by the Kaweah Colonists. Today Christmas services are held at high noon each Christmas day under the General Grant Tree.

It was not until 1914 that the military administration of the Sequoia and General Grant National Parks, created in 1890, was replaced by civilian administration. In 1940 the name of the area of which the General Grant Grove was a part was changed to Kings Canyon National Park.

The John Muir trail winds through the parks, past glaciers and deep-blue lakes, and through mighty forests. One of the surprises, about which nobody talks enough, is the beauty of the meadows filled with flowers, such as Crescent Meadow and Bearpaw Meadow. Villages are dotted along the Generals Highway, a continuation of State Highway 198. The parks have magnificent falls streaming down narrow gorges between steep slopes, excellent camping facilities, and many pleasant campground areas.

Death Valley National Monument

Today you can drive free and easy across the valley floor where half-starved forty-niners died of thirst. You can see the beauty to which their glazed eyes were blinded. The grim desert was first explored by prospectors who were looking for the lode of silver ore that one prospector found when he was looking for his lost gunsight. Nobody ever rediscovered the Lost Gunsight Mine, but they found silver and borax. Borax paid off for Aaron Winters, when he found deposits that were hauled away by twenty-mule teams.

The most dramatic person who ever came out of Death Valley was Death Valley Scotty, Walter Scott, who hit Los Angeles in 1905 with padlocked sacks of what he said was gold, and with many greenbacks that he scattered around. The story was that Scotty was a cowboy who had ridden in Buffalo Bill's Wild West Show. He said he had found a secret gold mine. Others knew he had a millionaire friend and that Scotty concocted the drama for laughs. The friends built a mansion that is now a museum. The elegant Provincial Spanish-style building was constructed at a cost of two million dollars.

Of Death Valley National Monument, established in 1933, some 550 square miles of the 2,981 square miles that comprise it are below sea level, the lowest level of the hemisphere. The eastern wall of the valley is formed by the Grapevine, Funeral, and Black Mountains. The western wall is the vivid Panamint Range. The Indians, because it was one of the hottest places in the region, named the valley Tomesha, "ground afire." It is not really a dead valley, for here bighorn sheep, coyote, wild burros, ground squirrels, kit foxes, and bushy-tailed antelopes know how to live.

The valley is a geologist's paradise. It was a lake at the end of the last glacial period, but the waters gradually evaporated. Rocks of all the great geological divisions of the earth's history are found here. Gold, silver, copper, and other minerals have also been found. Badwater, 279.6 feet below sea level, is the lowest point. Salty pools from the Amargosa River give the place its name.

Today the Death Valley Airport is opposite Furnace Creek Ranch, near the Visitors Center of this Natural Monument. The Devils Golf Course—a jumbled salt flat—is beside the highway near Furnace Creek Junction.

Joshua Tree National Monument

Joshua, who fought the battle of Jericho, gave the name to the trees that gave their name to this preserve. When Mormons came this way in the nineteenth century, they were reminded by the outstretched arms of the weird trees of Joshua at prayer.

The headquarters of the 870-square-mile monument is at Twenty Nine Palms in the Little San Bernardino Mountains. The preserve was dedicated to the National Park Service in 1936, in an effort to save some untouched desert. Lost Horse Valley and the Wonderland of Rocks have become famous.

GEOLOGY

Diverse is the word for the geology of California. Folded, fissured, faulted, the land was shaped by old seas and new earthquakes being born. The state has an area of 158,297 square miles. The shortest line from the Oregon border to Mexico is 780 miles long. The width of the state is from 150 to 350 miles. The line separating California from Nevada is arbitrary, but the Colorado River is the boundary between the southeastern region and Arizona.

The land once was bordered on both sides by the sea—the Pacific Ocean on the west and the Great Basin Sea of ancient times on the east. The oldest rocks are in the Sierra Nevada, a wrinkle in the earth's crust that tilts up sharply on the eastern edge and slopes gently to the west. Here, the most ancient rocks began as molten matter, magma, spewed up from the earth's interior, and metamorphic material changed by the heat of mountain building. The geological story of the area is of the raising, tilting, folding, and subsiding of the Sierra, where rivers carved the slopes of the west and deposited silts to the east. It was from the volcanic bedrock that gold was spewed up, and the streams that carried it down into rich gold sands. Volcanic activity has continued from age to age, with intermittent quiescence. In the Pleistocene epoch, recent geologically, the volcanos woke up again, and although they are dormant today, they are not dead. Mount Lassen in the Cascade Range still fumes actively.

In the last glacial period the ice fields marched forth, melted back, from millennium to millennium, carving deep canyons, making the lake basins, planing the slopes.

In the Coast Range, sedimentary rocks and limestone laid down under old seas are present. There are cretaceous rocks in abundance in the Coast Range, but the numerous beds of coal are of poor quality. Much organic siliceous shale was laid down all along the coast, becoming the source of the oil of California. Interior seas and bays veined the Coastal Range and spread far behind it.

One of the most important features of the structure of this land, periodically cracking and upheaving under interior stress, is the San Andreas Fault, which caused the San Francisco earthquake in 1906. It extends from forty miles north of San Francisco to the Imperial Valley, more than six hundred miles southeast. Other smaller faults include the Hayward Fault, parallel to the San Andreas, and several transverse faults that cut the Coast Range. There are many lesser faults.

As the mountains rose, through wrinkling of the earth's skin, they deposited in streams and rivers a vast load of sediment that filled the inland seas and bays to make the rich, level valleys of the state. In addition to the Coast Range and the Sierra, with their generally north-south trends, there are several transverse ranges—the Santa Ynez, Santa Monica, San Gabriel, and San Bernardino Mountains—with an east-west trend.

The Great Basin, east of the Sierra, is entirely desert except for the fertile soils under irrigation. The California deserts include the Colorado and the Mojave. There is evidence aplenty of dramatic changes that have occurred in recent times. Indian campsites are found beside what were once lakes and are now salt flats. The Salton Sea was a desert at the beginning of this century, until the Colorado River overflowed. Still there is evidence that it was an ancient sea.

Many areas of the state are rich in fossils, including the Mojave and Death Valley deserts, Inyo County's "oldest muds in the world," and the La Brea Pits in Los Angeles County. In numerous ancient caves in the northern part of the state many bones of mammals that were swept in by river floods ages ago have been found.

PLANT AND ANIMAL LIFE

Because California's climate ranges from the Arctic cold of perpetual snow to subtropical on the southern coast and arid desert in the interior, its plant and animal life is as widely diversified as its geology. Altitude is more important than latitude. The Sierra and the intervening deserts have acted as barriers between the state and the rest of the continent, so that many species are found here that live nowhere else in the world. Since the Ice Age, the two species of Sequoia and the Monterey cypress have been extinct everywhere else in the world.

The fertile soil and the benign climate make the land most hospitable to immigrants of the plant world. The Spanish settlers introduced the yellow mustard, which has gone wild and covers hillsides. Roses, geraniums, camellias, azaleas, begonias, bougainvillea, pepper trees, hibiscus, and many imported palms thrive in various areas, as well as the commercial fruit trees and berry vines.

The lakes, rivers, and coasts of California are rich in fish. The cool waters of the coast produce prolific life. The California lobster, the sardine, the abalone, oysters, clams, and scores of fish are important to commercial fishermen and to anglers.

California's grizzly bear is now extinct, but the tule elk has been preserved in a state park near Bakersfield and a preserve in Owens Valley. Other animals are the black-tailed deer, mule deer, black bear, Pacific weasel, skunk, fox, mountain beaver, California ring-tailed cat, bobcat, mountain lion, bighorn sheep, coyote, marten, badger, muskrat, and otter. Herds of sea lions loaf and roar on the rocks off the coast around San Francisco. Leopard seals are seen from time to time.

Californians love their outdoors and are historically enthusiastic in protecting it from despoliation by private interests. The result is that, of the state's land area of 100,314,000 acres, only about half is owned privately. About 47,000,000, almost 47 per cent, are owned by the federal government. Approximately 3,000,000 acres, three per cent, are state-owned. Private owners have about fifty per cent, approximately 50,000,000 acres.

Because such a large percentage of the state is in the hands of public agencies, it has proved easier than might otherwise have been the case to solve one of the major problems of certain parts of California. The problem is water—water for peoble, water for farms and groves. The northern part of the state flows with a wealth of water, the southern part—originally desertlike—is water poor. Water is carred to Los Angeles by a 238-mile-long aqueduct, the Owens River Aqueduct, and by the larger Colorado River Aqueduct. The Colorado River also helps to supply San Diego and the Imperial Valley. Some of the most ambitious water-control projects in the country are being carried out in California. The state adopted the first state-wide water plan in the country in 1957, and the voters approved a $1,150,000,000 bond issue to begin it in 1960. With 7,386,000 acres of irrigated farmland in California, the state has about twenty-two percent of such land in the country. A farsighted, competent handling of the state's water problems has been one of the evidences of the spirit that continues to make California great.

CLIMATE

California's greatest resource is probably its climate, which cannnot be exported—and this is true in spite of fog and smog. Floridians may find the state chilly, but certainly the temperature of all the state's coast is far more equable than that of other states to the east of the mountains on the same latitudes. Over-all, the climate is milder, and where it is hot, the lack of humidity helps. In the cooler northern regions, the fog acts as a blanket that helps to keep the earth warmer in winter, and also affords much of the moisture that causes the forests, ferns, and farms of that area to flourish. San Francisco's average low for a month, over a thirty-year period, was forty-nine degrees in January, and the average high was sixty-four degrees in September. San Diego, over the same thirty-year period, had an average low of fifty-five degrees in January and an average high of seventy-two degrees in August. That is not to say that extremes cannot be found in the state. The highest temperature in the United States was recorded in Death Valley on July 10, 1913, when the thermometer registered 134 degrees at Greenland

Ranch, 178 feet below sea level. The lowest temperature recorded in California was forty-five degrees below zero, registered at Boca, Nevada County, on January 20, 1937, at an elevation of 5,532 feet in the mountains.

ECONOMY

If the geology, geography, and climate of California are diverse, the economy is even more so. This diversity is, indeed, an economist's delight, because it has enabled the state to go from "boom to bust" and come out stronger, more thriving, richer, and more populous every time. A state where major industries include agriculture, oil production, tourism, movie making, and aircraft, satellite, and electronics manufacturing doesn't need to strike gold again. It would only confuse things. California today is the leading agricultural state in the country, and second to New York in manufacturing.

AGRICULTURE

To the fertility of the state's lands, today's farmers have brought water for irrigation and modern, mechanized, intensive farming. They have made California one of the country's major producers of fruits and vegetables, cotton and cattle, and many other products of the land. Agriculture is the most important industry in this most modern of American states. The long Central Valley, one of the world's most fertile regions, is the major growing area. Coastal valleys, the citrus area of Southern California, the irrigated Imperial valleys and slopes make up the rest of the state's agricultural lands.

In 1966, California exceeded all other states in cash receipts from farm marketing, with a $3,900,000,000 income. Iowa was second with $3,400,000,000 and Texas third with $2,100,000,000. California produces more eggs than any other state, 7,400,000,000 in 1966, compared to 4,500,000,000 from Georgia, the runner-up. The state's receipts from crops in 1966 totaled $2,310,000,000, as distinguished from livestock and poultry. That was tops in the United States. In livestock production the income was $1,600,000,000, second to Iowa. California was first in chickens and turkeys, third in sheep, fifth in cattle, in 1967.

California is the biggest vegetable-producing state in the country, second to Florida in oranges, third in potatoes. The state produces more grapes and raisins, peaches, pears, plums, prunes, lemons, apricots, figs, nectarines, sweet cherries, olives, dates, almonds, walnuts, sugarbeets, and tomatoes than any other state in the Union. Tomatoes are the top vegetable product, with lettuce second. Alfalfa and hay crops support the state's extensive dairy industry. A rare, tough-fibered cotton, Alcala, in great demand in making tires, has become an important crop, and California is the third state in cotton production.

Farm production increased more rapidly in the Pacific region than in any other part of the country in the 1960s, because of improved and mechanized methods of farming, improved varieties, improved irrigation, improved fertilizing, and soil improvement. In California, as in South Florida and Texas, twentieth-century machines have brought about a vast change in

122

vegetable production. Giant tractors and huge specialized plowing and harrowing machinery prepare the land. Some crops are seeded, fertilized, and sprayed from aircraft.

Wine is important economically to California today, with California wines dominating the market in the United States. This is the result of a good climate, a good soil, and a good variety of grape—plus skill and experimentation. Vineyards are cultivated in Napa and Sonoma counties, Fresno and Sacramento, and south to San Diego. Winemaking is steadily increasing, and the state produced 143,000,000 gallons in 1966. Though the first vineyards were planted in the nineteenth century, Prohibition was a setback. Many of the grape-growing regions today produce raisins, and California supplies raisins to almost all of the United States. Commercial winemaking was launched in California by the Hungarian Agoston Haraszthy, who brought 200,000 vine cuttings from Europe after he began planting his first vineyard in 1851. Dry wines come from the coastal area, with Alameda, Sonoma, and Napa counties leading in the production. Dessert wines are the specialty of the Central Valley. A grape festival and national wine show is held annually in September at Lodi, near Sacramento.

Periodically, as in 1968, the state faces labor crises in harvesting the crops; in that year it was table grapes that were causing the labor trouble. Agriculture had had the problem of getting sufficient pickers since the United States Congress in 1963 ended the employment of seasonal labor from Mexico on the theory that if farmers pay enough they can get unemployed United States citizens to harvest their crops.

COMMERCIAL FISHING

California is second to Alaska in commercial fishing, with a catch valued at $50,771,000 for 1966. Fish processing, canning, and freezing compose a substantial industry. Sea-food canning is important along the southern coast, for although Monterey's sardine crop has failed, tuna fish are in good supply.

MINERALS

Oil is the most important mineral produced in the state today, and has been for fifty years. California in 1966 was third in the country in production, with 61,661,000 barrels of crude petroleum, down a little from the preceding years of the decade. Texas was first and Louisiana second. Kern County, where oil was discovered in 1962, is the largest producer, with Los Angeles County second. The Brentwood Field, in Contra Costa County, is the northern limit of oil production. Los Angeles County is the refining center of the Pacific Coast and has sixteen refineries.

A wealth of oil lies under the ocean near the coast of California. This has been the subject of a struggle between the Federal government and the states. The Supreme Court said in 1945 that the Federal government owns all oil under the water from the shore to three miles out to sea. The Congress tried to reverse this decision by a law passed in 1952, and President Truman vetoed it. The Submerged Lands Act of 1953 gave the states all rights from the shore to three miles out and to the "seaward limit of inland waters." President Eisenhower signed that one. Thereupon, in 1963, California decided that this meant three miles beyond the Catalina Channel and the Channel Islands, considering them part of the main shoreline. The Supreme Court in 1965 said no to this. However, the rights of the state to the offshore bottom still extend three miles offshore under the Submerged Lands Act of 1953. Today, 996 offshore wells are producing and paying the state millions of dollars for the privilege of doing so. The oil output in 1966 was valued at $820,053,000, almost half the state's total mineral production.

In mineral production, California tops the country. Among other minerals coming from the earth are asbestos, boron, cement, diatomite, gypsum, mercury, rare-earth metals, sand and gravel, sodium sulfate, and tungsten. Some mining of metals is still carried on. There is tungsten ore in Inyo County. More than three million dollars' worth of gold was recovered, largely from placers, in 1962. This is done by dredging gravel out of river beds and by sluicing operations.

MANUFACTURING

California has solved the "long haul to market" problem, inherent in being distant from the centers of population, by *becoming* a major center of population. Manufacturing and industry have moved to where the people live who can man their plants and consume their products. Steel mills, aircraft-manufacturing plants, makers of durable goods, makers of transportation equipment, food processing, and makers of electrical machinery, ordnance, fabricated metal products, chemicals, and allied products all contribute significantly to the state's economy. Some of the most important missile-manufacturing and space-age hardware production is being done in California. Transportation equipment—under which title jets and missiles are classified— leads in importance in manufactured products. Food products, canned and frozen, are second. Electrical machinery, including electronic components, is third.

Today California's Douglas and Lockheed companies compete largely with Washington State's Boeing in the production of jet aircraft and missile components. They all vie for contracts for military and commercial aircraft of the future, including supersonic transports. They are all involved in the manufacturing of space-age vehicles. The dependence on assignments from the federal government, the vagaries of jet-age aircraft development and resultant contracts, make for a feast-and-famine existence to a degree, but not for long. The state's giant aerospace industries employ a third of all its manufacturing employees, estimated at close to two million people. California received $6,160,000,000 in defence and aerospace prime contracts in 1966, or 17.2 per cent of the total for the country.

RESEARCH

Much of the most important industrial work in California today results from the decision of the citizens of this state that they would be second to none in education. The California Institute of Technology is a result of that decision. In science, comparisons are odious, but Caltech has been a leader in theoretical physics for a generation, and that generation is the one that smashed the atom. California leads in nuclear power. The pioneer work in this field was done at the University of California by Dr. Ernest O. Lawrence, who built the cyclotron—the atom smasher. Lawrence, Dr. Glenn T. Seaborg, and their associates discovered plutonium and many radioactive isotopes used in medicine and industry.

Because California has the research facilities and the great men to man them, and because the state has the educational facilities to attract the bright young men needed to implement the findings of the scientists, nuclear physics is of prime importance on the Pacific Coast. Nuclear reactors have been built at La Jolla, Canoga Park, San Jose, and Pleasanton and near Los Angeles. Nuclear-powered plants are being used to generate electricity by three public utility firms. Ten per cent of the licenses of the Atomic Energy Commission have been granted in California. The first nuclear reactor to operate in outer space was built at Canoga Park by Atomics International and sent into space in 1966 from Vandenburg Air Force Base. The Jet Propulsion Laboratory of the California Institute of Technology designs and builds space-craft systems, maintains two-way communications with space craft, and analyzes scientific data obtained from flights. All this has meant many, many thousands of jobs for skilled Californians.

LABOR

Many of the men who had the gumption to make the trek west were skilled tradesmen among whom unions were being organized in the nineteenth century. California law in the 1860s was the first to ordain the eight-hour working day. The vigorous and independent pioneers handed on their heritage to the generations that have followed. San Francisco has been the trade-union center of California, and of the whole West, since early days.

All along the way there has been strife—first against pro-slavery adherents, then against the Chinese, then against the railroad and banking interests. The Coast Seamen's Union was organized in San Francisco in the 1880s. It is today the Sailor's Union of the Pacific. Then came the organization of waterfront workers, longshoremen, and their affiliates. The Knights of Labor flourished, along with the Workingmen's Party. The IWW (Industrial Workers of the World) came to the fore about 1913 in regard to field labor in the state, and helped to improve abjectly miserable conditions among migrant farm workers. Because of the anti-union campaigns in World War I, the labor movement faltered, and only regained strength in 1933. Unions arose and grew strong in the motion-picture industry. Today the fields and the vineyards are the battleground of the unionizing thrust. With all the improvement of workers' conditions, and all the growth of the economy, unemployment has not been eliminated in California, because of the population of the Pacific Coast.

POPULATION

The population estimate by the Bureau of the Census in 1964 was the first to give California first place in the nation, with 18,084,000 residents. New York State, which had been first since 1820, fell to second place. California also has the most cats and dogs, estimated at fifty million.

A measure of the rate at which California is growing is the increase in one decade, from 1950 to 1960, when the population grew 48.5 per cent.

No state is more cosmopolitan. Consider the figures: California's population in the 1960 census showed 15,717,204 people living in the state. Of these, 1,261,974 were "nonwhite." And of these "nonwhite," 883,861 were Negro, 39,014 were Indian, 157,317 were Japanese (more than any other state except Hawaii), and 95,600 were Chinese (more than any other state and twice as as many as Hawaii). There were more Filipinos, 65,459, than in any state except Hawaii. In California lived 1,343,686 foreign-born, more than any state except New York. Mexico made the largest contribution to the foreign-born, and Canada, England, Italy, and Germany followed in that order.

And though the state is the most populous in the nation, population density is comparatively low at 100.4 people per square mile, compared to 12,442.33 per square mile in the District of Columbia and 819.3 per square mile in Rhode Island, the most densely populated state.

ENVOI

From the metal poetry of the San Francisco Bay bridges, to the miracle of falling water at Yosemite, to the lunar shore of Mono Lake, to the pigmented hills in Death Valley National Monument, there are things to see and savor.

California has grown rapidly, in places far too rapidly, and the billboards and the ticky-tacky are monuments to haste and poor planning and bad taste.

But there are many faces of California, and beyond the hills of the frame-house horrors there are fields where young horses play and vines offer amber grapes in a sun sacrifice and the homes are small and happy and wreathed with charm.

California is a state of happy traveling. There is an endless procession of roads, from giant eight-lane freeways that boldly conquer the mountains, to quiet byways that follow the contour of the land and nod to the thickets of black oak and bundles of roadside redbud and sea-pointing rhododendrons. California's roads are excellent, and the lands they lead to are enough to please an explorer for a lifetime. Take the little roads to Bodie and Surprise Valley and Peanut and Paradise and Eshom Creek and Idyllwild and Anza. Each has a visual story to relate, and to listen is to be reassured.

The people in California are friendly—they'll take the time to talk, to answer questions, to point out directions to a local landmark. Many of them have come here since World War II, and they bring the homeyness of their former state or country with them.

To find California's Indians today, you must look hard. They are there, but they are woven into the pattern of population. Only on a few reservations will you find them living apart. All are proud people.

The people who have come to California since the days of the Spanish have given it much —cities and bridges and parks and science and industry. Poets have built their verse here, and novelists have run out the adventures of their characters on California streets. Artists have seen California and have molded it in stone and oil and metal.

Hollywood is a microcosm and the star system is changed. You are more apt to see a TV or motion picture personality at a hamburger stand or a gas station than walking down Sunset Boulevard.

California is smoke and steam and jet thunder and the din of a thousand cars on a freeway. It is wind tiptoeing along the tops of the coastal redwoods, water hammering at the older rocks in the deep Yuba River, pikas calling in the Sierra Nevada, sea lions honking off San Simeon.

California cannot be described simply. It is personal, quicksilver, exuberant, and almost without end. No man who has called here can ever put the myriad impressions out of his mind.

ACKNOWLEDGMENTS

In my book *San Francisco* I wrote, "Books being what they are, they belong as much to the local teller of tales as to the published author." The local tellers of this book on California were Russ Leadabrand, Edith Alt, Jack and Helen O'Leary, Herb Caen, Gitta Duke, Ed and Ruza Stackhouse, Dick Laugharn, Curt Gentry, Henry Berrey, and quite a few authors of books written before this one.

Although I took ninety-five per cent of the photographs, a few were supplied by my wife Ilse and my son Michael; by Edith Pegel Neidhardt, and by the Union Pacific Railroad; the fine airviews of San Francisco were provided by J. E. McWayne of United Air Lines. T. O'Conor Sloane III, the Doubleday editor of the book, gave editorial assistance.

I express my gratitude to all.

Hans W. Hannau